F
Adopticon Constellation

"My husband and I adopted a son over twenty years ago, and I wish I'd had this book to read ahead of him coming home with us. Terri explains beautifully yet painfully what it really is like for adopted children, perhaps especially if the child is older when adopted. It can be a joyous occasion for the adoptive parents yet bewilderingly painful for the child. Thank you, Terri, for your honest approach to your book."
    —Beth Staff BS, MS, author of *Auggie's Neigh Neigh*

"My husband was adopted in 1963, and the records were sealed. We adopted our younger son in 2010, and we regularly meet with his birth family. Primal wound theory is real and visits my family in surprising ways at varying degrees. Now that I have the open book that is Terri Decker's heart, I feel better prepared to care for my husband and child."
    —Jody Dyer, author of *The Eye of Adoption: A Turbulent True Story of Heartache, Humor, & Hope*

"'Stranger than fiction' yet brutally authentic, Decker tells the story of her relinquishment and the complexities of its ever-unfolding aftermath while drawing us to the many characters involved with a genuine and bewildering sense of compassion. As an adoptive parent, *Adoption Constellation* is a must read.

The courageous writing left me questioning my limited perspective and what I may be taking for granted in our own adoption story."

—Patricia Lombardi

"Terri Decker's courageously personal memoir represents a much-needed addition to the body of literature available on adoption today. Her experiences as an adoptee and as an adoptive parent, combined with her reflections on attachment and familial interconnectedness, powerfully demonstrate the social and psychological challenges that accompany adoption. Terri is able to show that beauty and intimacy can result, in spite of these challenges, if we understand adoption as a lifelong process of reflection, conversation, questions and insights. A must-read for anyone who is touched by adoption, personally or professionally."

—Martin Srajek PhD, LCSW

"*Adoption Constellation: A memoir of Being Adopted and Adopting* is a jewel that is sure to become a popular resource for people looking into adoption or wanted to understand their own emotions about their own adoption. This type of work is born out of pain and an eventual understanding of what it means for a child to be given to another person to be raised. Terri understands both sides of this issue, and which clarity and caring, she is able to guide and explain the journey." —Karen Eyman Kinder, LCPC, LMHC, CSAT, CMAT

Adoption Constellation

A Memoir of Being Adopted and Adopting

Terri Decker

crippledbeaglepublishing.com

Instagram: adoption_constellation
Facebook: Terri Miller-Decker

Cover design by Lauren Harris

Scriptures marked NLT are taken from the HOLY BIBLE, NEW LIVING TRANSLATION (NLT): Scriptures taken from the HOLY BIBLE, NEW LIVING TRANSLATION, Copyright© 1996, 2004, 2007 by Tyndale House Foundation. Used by permission of Tyndale House Publishers, Inc., Carol Stream, Illinois 60188. All rights reserved. Used by permission.

Paperback ISBN 978-1-958533-04-8
Hardcover ISBN 978-1-958533-05-5

Library of Congress Control Number: 2022916128

In a contemporary memoir, stories are told as the author can best recall. Dialogue, events, and dates in this life story are as accurate as possible given the frailties of the human memory. Names have been changed to protect individuals' privacy. Regardless, the soul is the soul, and the author prays that readers understand her message.

Published and printed in the United States of America.

A recurring dream
Wakes me
In the middle of the night

Deep in sleep
Then awakened

Someone is knocking
On my bedroom door

It sounds like
My bedroom door...
Is it?

I lie still
Eyes open
Holding my breath
Waiting
For the knock
To come again

Waiting to hear the voice
Of one of my children
But none comes

It's perplexing
It cannot be a knock
I hear in my dream
It's too real
And present

Who is it
That wants to come in?

Why do they knock
And go away?

It occurs to me:
Maybe
It's not someone
Wanting to come in...
Maybe...
It's someone knocking
Wanting to get out

She comes knocking
In the stillness of the night
When my thoughts,
My will,
The noise of life,
Have all been quieted
When my defenses
Are completely down

She is asking to be freed;
Asking for permission
To be released from years
Of forced slumber
And silent waiting
In her resolute acquiescence
She was forgotten
The idea of her existence...
Abandoned...
Until...
She came knocking

She must return

And keep knocking
For me to believe
In her existence
To Believe, that she indeed,
Wants to emerge from her place
Of safety

There has been Safety in silence
Which is now
Threatened
As she knocks,
Seeking to be heard,
To be freed

Sorrow prepares you for joy. It violently sweeps everything out of your house, so that new joy can find space to enter.

It shakes the yellow leaves from the bough of your heart, so that fresh, green leaves can grow in their place.

It pulls up the rotten roots, so that new roots hidden beneath have room to grow. Whatever sorrow shakes from your heart, far better things will take their place.

~ Rumi

A Day Like No Other

One of my earliest memories is of standing and looking out the front door of what I recall being a long, brick building. To someone else, the passageway might appear rather benign, but this was no ordinary door. It symbolized miles of separation; an end to one life and the beginning of another, neither of which offered me a choice. As I gazed out, I was looking without really seeing, yet longing for a familiar car to come driving up the gravel road to the orphanage. I was waiting for my mother to come and get me.

This is the story of my relinquishment and adoption. Many of the puzzle pieces are still missing, so I can only imagine how I, then a two-year-old, might have felt while living through this traumatic event. If you thought adoptions were simply joyful, precious, and celebratory (which they can be), then you have considered them only from one perspective—the adoptive parents' perspective. From the vantage point of the adopted child, you may envision a myriad of emotions, questions, and doubts. A child is simply *connected* to his or her parent(s), and from his or her perspective there is no logical explanation for being *separated* from this solid, natural foundation. This foundation is not just part of the child but actually is the child. This relationship is not one that is replaced as easily as tossing old shoes and buying new. Even with its imperfections, the bond fits perfectly because

13

the bond was designed that way from the beginning. Separation is like being ripped apart from the inside out; there are no words to describe it. There are only deeply held feelings that sometimes cannot be explained. There are questions and doubts that surround your very being. "Why did they leave me? What's wrong with me? Why didn't they want me?"

Your views of yourself and the world suddenly change. Not only is your own self-worth brought into question, but also the safety of the world around you is uncertain. Who can be trusted now if one's own parents cannot be trusted to be present?

As an adoptee, I look at life differently. Throughout life, the doubt in my mind often made me feel like I was living in a nightmare and would never wake up. I was on guard. I was vigilant. I had a jaded outlook.

What little information I have about my early life was given to me in a short letter from my birthmother. I first contacted and met her in 1994 (thirty-one years after my adoption). Nine years after that initial meeting, I was finally able to ask her questions about our history together. I didn't want to upset her or lay blame or guilt on her. I didn't want her to be disappointed with me (again). I'm not sure I had the right to ask any questions at all, and she was not forthcoming with information on her own. Her answers were sketchy and brief, not the detailed descriptions I hoped for. The skeletal facts comprised only a few paragraphs of a three-and-a-half-page letter. At the conclusion, she asked that I burn the letter after reading it. Of course, I kept it. The letter is my history, pieces of a puzzle buried for too long.

Burning it was out of the question. I learned from her letter that she was a wild, self-destructive teenager looking to get away from home any way possible. At the age of seventeen, she gave birth to my brother.

Two years later, I was born. Our father was around for only a short time; he and my mother didn't get along. She attributes this mainly to her own hardheadedness. It's likely that my father never laid eyes on me. My birthmother did her best, I believe, to raise my brother and me. She worked, and our maternal grandmother watched us with the help of an aunt, one of my mother's three sisters. Life was barely manageable for this young mother, and then illness hit the family. The aunt who helped watch us became ill with cancer. (She passed away a few years after we were adopted.)

During that time, our mother decided to give my brother and me up for adoption. I was barely two, and my brother was four. Our father had not been helpful or around for some time. Even though his name was said to be listed on my birth certificate, I doubt he signed (or was even required to in the sixties) any relinquishment papers. What transpired those few months and weeks before we were sent to the children's home is a mystery. I can only imagine the scene.

March, that time of year when winter is over but spring hasn't quite arrived, a time when change is in the air. You can breathe its newness, its promise of growth. There are signs of spring and change outside. The snow is gone and an occasional patch of green pops up from the barren ground.

Things seem different at home too. Change must be coming our way. Grandma sits with me more often, which is a lot since we love to rock and read books. I am warm and safe with her in her rocking chair. There aren't as many early-morning arguments in the kitchen. Yes, change is coming, and for right now, it seems to be a good thing. The smell of coffee fills the morning air. Aunts, uncles, and cousins mill about the house. A party? But the mood is somber. There's a lot of whispering, with extra hugs and kisses going around.

My brother and I are magnets for most of the affection. I don't mind at all. This is a place of belonging. The coffee pot is filled and emptied numerous times, and then, one by one, family members leave, giving my brother and me what seem to be super-long hugs. There are a few tears too, and I'm not sure why. It's only grandpa, grandma, and mom left with us now. Mom pulls us in close and begins to talk to us. She is direct and to the point. I understand every word but don't like what I'm hearing.

"You're going to have a new mommy and daddy."

What could she possibly be talking about? Why would I get a new mommy? Why would I even want one? This is home. I belong here and nowhere else. Confusion creeps in. There is a knock at the door, and a strange man is welcomed in. Everyone else knows him. I hear talk about being ready and a long car ride. I'm not sure who's going on this car ride, but I don't plan on going anywhere. I climb up into my grandmother's lap. More pleasantries are exchanged, and then the strange man says, "It's time." All eyes are directed at my brother and me and panic slowly overtakes me. The scene comes together but makes no sense at all. I put a death grip on my grandmother's neck with my arms, hoping to hear her tell me not to worry, that I'm not going anywhere. Only half of my hopes are realized. She tells me not to worry, I will be just fine, and I'll have a new home.

The strange man with the hat picks me up as I try to squirm free from his grasp. Nothing works and yet I continue pushing against him stiff-armed, my knees digging into his chest. I take a hard dive to one side in another attempt to free myself, but he is quick and grabs me, pulling me back, increasing his hold on me. His tight grip is exhausting as I continue to push against him all the way down the sidewalk to the waiting car. As the man opens the car door, Carl climbs up on the seat. He has given in before the car is even started. The man drops me on the seat next to Carl and closes the door. I immediately jump to my feet and begin looking out the back window. The house already appears smaller, even though we have not even moved an inch away. The man is talking, but I'm not listening. I'm focused on the house, hoping someone will open the door and come running to the car to get me. The door never opens. We pull away, and the house soon disappears.

I cannot imagine how my mother and grandparents were able to get me from the house into the stranger's car or how that last "good-bye" might have been. I envision the scene from inside the car, then while standing in the backseat, then from the street, as an adult, watching the car pull away with a frightened toddler looking out the back window. I see her little hand pressed against the glass. Her fear, rage, questions, and uncertainty are locked inside the soundproof car.

The Orphanage

I don't remember that car ride from Michigan to Indiana or the arrival at the children's home, but I do remember a long, brick building. On our way back from Michigan several years ago, Mark (my husband) and I took a detour and drove by the orphanage property. The orphanage is still there but functions in a different capacity than it did forty-eight years ago. We drove through a rather flat, rural area to where the home is spread across several acres. My memory was correct. We drove up to a long, brick building. I felt a tightening in my gut, a slowing of my breathing, as we eased to a stop. There were no words, just a heaviness with the realization that someone had once sent me here.

My adoptive mother told me that the children's home hurried to move us through the system and find us a permanent family. The home was already beyond capacity when we arrived, and the state was breathing down their necks to stay within licensing limits.

This is probably a good place to talk about my vague hints at former abuse. For some reason, as I grew up, I always had suspicions that sexual abuse was somehow part of my past. I had no recollection of specific incidents, so I was baffled as to why I thought that something had happened. I never talked about or mentioned this idea to anyone. Later in life, during a therapy session, I finally let out the buried suspicions of abuse. Nothing ever materialized from the discussion, but I was relieved to tell someone what had secretly nagged at me for decades.

A year or more later, I was searching for people in my past who might have the missing pieces of my "life puzzle." One such person was the superintendent of the orphanage. I singled him out because I had learned from asking my adoptive parents more questions that he was likely the man who came to my home and brought me to the orphanage. My adoptive mother believed that he was a friend of my biological family.

As I began searching his name and the name of the orphanage, I discovered that a lawsuit alleging sexual abuse by at least two of the employees had been filed against the orphanage. One of the accused was the home's minister (this particular orphanage, or children's home, was run by a non-denominational church), and the other was the superintendent who had taken me to the orphanage. I read, with my heart pounding in disbelief.

The accusations were atrocious. I purposefully omit the names of these victims and the organization because I have no desire to cause them any more anguish than they have already experienced. Suffice it to say, the allegations were true. In an August 24, 2001, phone interview with Indiana newspaper *Post-Tribune*, the minister admitted his guilt. Could this be where the haunting feelings of abuse originated? Even if I were not the victim of such abuse, clearly, I was in an unsafe environment. I wonder what I might have sensed at the tender age of two. I was already distraught and frightened after being taken away from my family. To be in an unfamiliar environment where children were being abused must have only compounded the nightmare I was living.

A few years after Mark and I drove by the property, I made a call to the children's home and asked if I could visit. I was hoping to find some records, pictures, anything. Even the smallest piece of information was (is) important and can add a missing puzzle piece to my life. When I made the call and subsequent visit, I had no idea of the allegations that had been made several years earlier.

Walking into the building, I felt uneasy. The decor was dated, with wall-to-wall carpeting and paneled walls. After the three-hour drive, I needed a quick stop in the restroom. There, I wondered if I had been in the tiny room before. To think that I had walked the same floors forty-five years ago as a small child mourning the loss of her family was numbing. I assumed I would feel something profoundly deep, yet the moment was surreal— (not in a good way). The staff members I met were pleasant, but I felt I was intruding and had no right to be there looking for anything. The visit was futile. I found nothing. The business manager offered to search old records after I left, but uncovered nothing. It was as if my brother and I were phantoms. We *were* there, but my only proof is a typed letter from the director to my adoptive parents. No other records exist.

Growing up: Coming "Home" From the Orphanage

I always felt I had a "normal" family growing up. Except for the fact that five of the six children in our family were adopted (with the occasional foster child), we were just like every other family. I now know there is absolutely nothing "normal" about having five adopted children, especially when some of those children were severely wounded upon arrival. Being abandoned, placed for adoption, call it what you will, is wounding enough. When emotional, physical, or sexual abuse is added to the abandonment, the wound is exacerbated. I never remember talking about my adoption. I always knew that I was adopted, and I knew the story of the day my adoptive parents brought me home, but beyond that, it was not a topic of discussion in our family. Ever.

Still, being adopted was always on my mind. There was rarely a night that I didn't lie in bed and think about my birthmother. Questions ran through my mind: *Where is she? What is she doing? Why didn't she want me?* These were followed by thoughts like, *I don't really want to know her anyway*, or *I wonder if she will come looking for me someday*, and, *I'm sure she has lots of money and will come and take me back*. The question that permeated my soul, but I never voiced was, *What's wrong with me?*

Obviously, there is something inherently wrong and unnatural for a mother not to want her child.

Compounding the wounds of abandonment are the emotions associated with it. Often, those emotions are locked away inside, the adoptee never letting on that there might be a myriad of tangled emotions buried deep beneath the surface. Not only did I hide these questions and worries from those around me, but I also convinced myself that I had no complications or issues with my relinquishment and adoption. I often told myself: "I'm fine. It's God's will. My adoption was 'meant to be.'"

Only recently did I ask my mother to fill in more details about bringing my brother and me home for the first time. Sometime in late February or early March, we were taken to the children's home. I was two years old. My brother was four. With more than one hundred children, the home was overcrowded. The boys and girls had separate "homes." That meant my brother and I didn't get to interact. We were in the orphanage for about a month when my soon-to-be adoptive parents came for a visit. They wanted to expand their family but had been unable to conceive.

Then, a fortuitous call came to their minister. The caller gave the minister information about siblings who were available for immediate adoption. Letters of referral were written, and soon after, my parents made the trip to Indiana to meet us.

Kids, kids, everywhere. I liked it better in my own home, where there were fewer kids and I knew the routine, even if that meant being at my grandma's house one day and my aunt's the next. At least I knew the people I was with. I don't know anyone here; there are lots of kids and very few moms and dads. Everything is "long." A long car-ride here, down a long, tree-lined road, to a long, brick building, sleeping in a long hall lined with beds; everything a long way from home. I stood at the door again today watching and waiting for my mom to come back. I hope she knows where to find me; I wonder if I've had this "new mom and dad" long enough.

Maybe my mom's ready to come back and get us. As I stand gazing and waiting, the sun slowly warms my face. The warmer weather prompts one of the moms to take all the kids outside. Before I know it, my coat is on, and one of the big girls is holding my hand, leading me out into the sunshine.

My coat is two sizes too big for me. Even when I raise my arms, my hands don't peek out from my sleeves. I don't mind since it keeps me warm. The play area is just behind the long, brick building. It's a large grassy area with a tall silver swing set that has six places to sit. Just behind the swing set is a wide dirt field that looks like it could stretch on forever.

The swings are all taken, so I wander over to the small orchard that divides the brick building from the little white church where we go every Sunday. The sun is slowly melting the frost off the grass. I squat down and watch, mesmerized by the melting. Tiny droplets make their way down the blade of grass, like teardrops falling down a face. The grass is crying; I want to cry forever, but the tears don't work. They don't bring my mother back. As another drop of water begins to fall down the blade of grass, a red rubber ball comes rolling to a stop right in front of me. Picking it up is a challenge since my hands can't find their way out of the sleeves. Just as I manage to pick up the ball between my coat sleeves, a tall boy takes it away, saying, "Thank you." Tears form and begin a quick descent down my face. I can't hold on to anything, not my family, my mom, or even a playground ball.

I find a seat on a small stump and watch all the activity around me. It's just a blur of motion and jumbled noise. I'm looking past it all, wondering, waiting, sad. One of the moms says, "It's time for lunch," and the ground begins to tremble from the rush of feet running to the door. I sit on my stump and wait, afraid of being run over by all the older kids. Carl runs too, trailing behind the stampede and grinning with delight. I don't know how he can be so happy when we are so far from home.

As the line of kids slowly shrinks and disappears inside, I stand up and wander over to the steps leading to the door. I focus on one large step at a time. I'm more interested in the sound of my feet hitting the concrete than the lunch that's waiting for me. Once inside, we make the walk down the long hallway lined with beds. I keep my focus on my shoes, watching as I step on each tile, first a light one, then a dark one. It looks like one giant checkerboard. Keeping up with the mom with cat-eyed glasses isn't too difficult. She walks slowly, letting me go at my own pace as I step on each alternately colored tile. Dark, light, dark, light ... all the way down the hall. I don't look up until we reach the last bed—mine. It's neatly made with a yellow flowered bedspread. One of the big girls made the bed this morning and left her white, furry, stuffed cat resting at the foot. The mom with the cat-eyed glasses pulls out a chair for me in the large eating room.

I climb up and hear the big girl next to me say, "April Fool's." I don't really know what this means except that

24

kids are saying things that aren't true and then saying "April Fool's."

"Look, there's a spider on your coat. April Fool's." "Hey, look at that monkey. April Fool's." I hear this several times from big kids as we eat our lunch of macaroni and cheese, apple slices, jiggly red Jell-O, and a cookie. I eat a few bites of the macaroni and cheese, all of the jiggly red Jell-O, and one bite of my cookie. I fill up quickly, watching as the other kids eat their lunches and one by one take their plates to the big tub for dirty dishes. Then we all go back to the long room with our beds.

Normally after lunch, we have rest time, but today the man with the hat tells us that he wants us to meet someone. Our "new mommy and daddy are coming to visit" us. I hear "mommy" and "visit" and know that she has finally found her way here to take us back home. I am eager to take his hand this time and follow his lead down the hall. Carl has the man's other hand and of course is still grinning. I haven't allowed myself even a hint of a smile. I'm much too cautious, even at the tender age of two. I walk with anxiety, eager to be in my mom's arms once again.

As I walk back into the room that was full of noisy children eating their lunches just minutes before, I scan from one corner to the other to find my mother. She's not here, but there are three strangers in the room. A man, a woman, and a girl who is bigger than my brother. Where is my mother? The woman has short, dark brown hair that is a little poofy on top. The man is quiet, with dark curly hair. The girl is quiet too and eying us carefully. Her hair is dark and thick just like her parents' and falls to her shoulders.

Carl immediately climbs onto the man's lap and says, "I'm going home with you."

The woman speaks first, "Hi Terri. I like your dress."
I look down at my shoes and say nothing. I can't understand
why Carl is so friendly with these strangers and wants to go
home with them. The frown on my face is permanently set.
"You're not too sure about us, are you?" the woman says.
Again, I remain silent, wondering where my mother is.
The man with the hat sits down, and there is talk about
"waiting" and "foster home." I don't know what any of this
is about. I keep my distance and my frown. Their chatter
goes on and on, so I wander from chair to chair, running my
hands across the plastic covering each one. Each time the
woman or man tries to get my attention, I move farther away.
I want nothing to do with these strangers. Their talk and
attempts to engage me don't stop. Then the man with the hat
says, "Terri, you are going home with your new mom and
dad today."

My adoptive mother told me that I spoke in more complete sentences than my brother, two years my senior. My mantra was, "No, get your hands off me." I was not a charming and endearing two-year-old, yet they decided to take my brother and me home that day. Their lawyer advised against it, but the orphanage was looking to put us in a foster home within the week. No one wanted us to go through another placement and separation. It was April Fool's Day, and the story I heard many times was that on the car ride to my new home, I repeated my mantra and threw up red Jell-O all over my new six-year-old sister. The emotional trauma of being sent off with complete strangers had nowhere to go but up and out.

The swift expansion of the family put my adoptive mom in a frenzy to make arrangements for her part-time job as a school bookkeeper. The school district she worked for was accommodating and let her do the books at home. That next morning at breakfast she asked me if I wanted cereal. I cried. Actually, I screamed. She took it away. "Toast?"

More screaming.

"Cereal again?"

I took it, but still was not happy.

"Milk?"

More screaming. Finally, I accepted milk with the original cereal. What I probably wanted was the familiarity of my family of origin. I just wanted to be taken home. I believe I was letting her know that I wanted neither this breakfast nor this new family.

My brother was easier to please and smiled all the time. He couldn't sit still. My mother remembers that he was into everything. I loved to be read to, but he didn't have the attention span to sit and listen, so mom chased him around during times she could have read to me. She lost about twenty pounds those first couple of months.

I have only a few memories of my first few years adjusting to a new family. Two memories involve cats.

Curiosity was getting the best of me. The small hole, the size of a bottle cap, in the closet floor kept getting my attention. Two of my four-year-old fingers slid in easily. What was beyond where my fingers could reach? A dried macaroni noodle from my Sunday school art paper dropped in without a sound.

Next, I tried a pencil, three red beads, a straw, the bottle from a Tiny Tears doll, and a metal pincer from the bathroom. They all disappeared without a sound. The squishy ball started to go in but got stuck. When I tried to pull it out, a piece of the floor began to pull up with it. I discovered a little door in the floor! The ball slipped from my grasp and the door shut with a muffled thud.
Determined to see what was beneath the magic door, I got a better grasp and slowly lifted.

I peeked into the spooky darkness as two green eyes returned my stare. Frightened is an understatement. I had no idea that a cat's eyes could glow like that. I immediately dropped the tile and screamed, trying to catch my breath. The cat was black and belonged to us, but I never expected to see only its eyes suspended in midair, staring at me from beneath the floor.

My haunting experience, however, did not keep me from my curiosity toward felines. Our neighbors two houses away also had cats. Lots of cats. My guess is fifteen, but I was four years old, and life and its memories exist in quantum proportions. Visiting their home was always an adventure for two reasons: one, they had lots and lots of cats, and two, the man who lived there could take out his teeth. It appeared to me that he swallowed them only to bring them back up into his mouth where they belonged. I was intrigued and mystified by this magical phenomenon. Of course, I never remember anyone explaining to me the concept of dentures. Many of their cats were Siamese. My experience with Siamese cats is that they are temperamental and fond only of their owners, and even that is subject to the cats' moods at any given moment. My sister's family later owned a Siamese cat they called *Sugar*. Sugar was the meanest cat I've ever met. He would come tearing into a room and attack for no reason. *Demon* would have been a more fitting name.

One particular visit probably sealed my disdain for the furry animals. For some reason, most, if not all, of the cats were in the laundry room. They must have liked its warmth and coziness. I entered as the hum of the dryer and whirring washing machine kept in rhythm with one another. The cats perched, sitting one by one, at attention atop the washer, dryer, and folding table. The meanest cat in the bunch (of course, Siamese) was named Nankypoo. Nankypoo was not to be meddled with, but for some reason, I wanted to figure out which cat was Nankypoo. I began to ask. I started at one end of the room, stood directly in front of each cat, and asked, "Are you Nankypoo?" I passed from cat to cat, getting no response at all. I looked boldly and directly into each cat's eyes, demanding to know which one would claim the name. Not one of them budged until I came to the real Nankypoo.

As soon as I asked him if he owned up to the name, he reached out with one swipe of his paw and gave me a powerful answer that resulted in a scar across my eyelid. I ran from the room crying and hollering about my newly inflicted wounds. Nankypoo had made himself known!

The last memory I have from this time period is having my mouth washed out with soap. I had asked my mother for some wax paper. My plan was to rub it on our slide to make the rides down fast paced and exciting. For some reason, she denied my request. I then complained to whomever was outside waiting for me to bring the wax paper. I fumed, "She won't give me any." Unbeknownst to me, the windows were open, and she heard my grumblings. She promptly called me back in the house and washed my mouth out with soap. I believe I learned my "lesson." I learned not to voice discontent, anger, disagreement, or opinions in general.

A Growing Family

We moved from Fairbury, Illinois, a rural farming community to the town of Normal. I consider myself fortunate to have lived in the same town for all of my grammar and high school years. Our family began growing again when I was in the second grade. I wrote about the wish to have a baby brother in one of my school assignments, but little did I know my wish would come true so quickly. My mother worked as a secretary at a local grade school where children from The Baby Fold attended. This was a home for orphaned and dependent children.

One such boy frequented the school office. Mom found out that he would soon be sent to a group foster home if a permanent family was not found for him. The Baby Fold was diligent in seeking a secure home, but each attempt ended with the same result. He was sent back. The prospects were bleak. He hadn't been sent back two or three times, but fourteen. Rejected, fourteen times! Imagine what that would do to you, what it would say about who you are, your worth and "wanted-ness."

Trent made his first visit on a Saturday, and we went to a local park. I remember that it went well except that he didn't want to go back to The Baby Fold. Shortly after, though, he moved in with us. He was sixteen months younger than I was, not really the "baby" I was hoping for, but a younger brother, nonetheless. Trent's first meal with us was memorable.

All was well until it was time to clear our plates from the table. We were each responsible for rinsing our plate and putting it in the dishwasher. Trent wasn't about to partake in such a ritual. The battle was on.

I learned early to be compliant (at least this is my recollection), so I had no idea that one could put up such a battle with a parent and survive! As he proceeded to walk away from the table and his plate, mom grabbed him around his midsection pulling him back toward his responsibilities still sitting on the table. He began pawing for anything stationary that would give him a foothold. The refrigerator door gave him a temporary reprieve until the door came flying open. I stood with wide-eyed amazement, observing the ensuing battle from a safe distance.

The remaining details are fuzzy, but I'm pretty sure he cleaned his plate and put it in the dishwasher. I was not as successful when it came to winning a battle with him. I only remember one altercation.

School was out for the summer. I had just completed fourth grade and Trent third. The early summer day was perfect. Not too hot, the day was just right for an afternoon of one-on-one wiffle ball in the back yard. Trent pitched. I batted.

"That was a perfect pitch!" he shouted, as I let it go and tossed it back.

"It was outside," I said.

"What was wrong with that one?" He asked, as I let another one sail by.

"Too high." I tossed it back and it went over his head.

"You just can't hit my pitching, and you know it!"

"You just can't pitch. C'mon, give me a good one."

The next pitch was exactly where I wanted it. The black plastic bat connected with the ball in just the right spot and sent a line drive into the crabapple tree.

"Yes!" I shouted as I tapped the air conditioner (first base). Stepping on the shirt that marked second base, I noticed that the ball was taking its time rolling down the tree branches. Trent glanced at me when I zipped past him to the peach tree (third base).

"You have to go back to second. The ball is stuck," he said as it finally hits the ground.

I slowed down to a trot as I headed to home plate. "Nope, it's an in-the-park home run, and I CAN hit your pitching!" I shouted over my shoulder. The sound of running feet got closer, but I didn't turn fast enough. Before I knew it, I was flat on my back. Trent had me pinned and glared into my eyes. "Get off of me," I said, burning with anger at him and myself for letting him catch me off guard. I tried loosening his grip with a quick jerk of my body but to no avail.

His contemptuous gaze was cold and constant. He said nothing, knowing I was at his mercy. Finally, he released his grasp and let me go.

I was a tomboy who played ball with the guys in the neighborhood and considered myself just as strong as any of them. I was no pushover and certainly not used to being flattened. I learned to steer clear of him.

Not until my freshman year of high school did our family once again began to grow. This time it was a six-year-old girl. Cathy had mild cerebral palsy, which mostly affected her speech. I had to listen very closely to discern her words. With time and speech therapy, she was easier to understand. Not too long after her arrival, a seven- year-old boy, Neal, also joined our family. He had a full head of wild curly hair and a contagious laugh. Cathy and Neal had their adoptions finalized on the same day, making our family of eight now complete. Mary, the oldest and only biological child, had already left home for college. Carl (my biological brother) left home before he finished high school. Trent and Neal followed in his footsteps.

My memories of grade school and junior high are few. I do remember the torture of having to watch my brothers play baseball. I wanted to be out on the field making plays and getting base hits. Instead, I had to watch them play tentatively, usually striking out at the plate. High school was bearable because, finally, I played competitive sports. Every season brought a new opportunity to exert my energy. I played softball, basketball, and my favorite, volleyball. Somehow, my freshman year I also managed to squeeze in tennis.

I would characterize my adopted siblings as "troubled" children. The "trouble" ranged from setting fires to challenging authority to having difficulties in school to acting out sexually. I worked hard to be the "good kid." I was a rule follower (mostly). On the rare occasion that I did not follow the rules, I flew under the radar. I may have been subconsciously wishing that I could be a rebel, a rule-breaker, which is probably why I was a bit of a prankster. I pulled my most daring prank on my high school P.E. teacher.

There were actually two teachers involved. One, Mr. Logan, had a military background and was not someone to cross. The other, the one the prank was intended for, was Mr. Frank. He was laid back, easygoing, and we enjoyed a good rapport.

The gym and hallway to the locker room were quiet. All the students were outside on the track, some jogging around like they were supposed to. I was in search of props for my prank. High on the closet shelf in the teacher's office was a yellow plastic bucket. It was perfect. The bucket must have been a child's beach bucket at one time. It was light enough to rest on the top of the partially opened door yet would hold enough water to thoroughly soak an unsuspecting teacher. There was an abundance of string and tape in the closet as well. Starting at the desk where I would be sitting, I carefully taped the string to the cement wall, over the closet door, on top of the door frame, and then I saved string to tie to the white handle. The bucket of water was now in place and tied to the string.

I waited a bit nervously for the door to open. The door finally began to move, and I pulled the string attached to the bucket while simultaneously being hit with a wave of panic and dread. It wasn't the jovial Mr. Frank who walked in, but rather the drill sergeant Mr. Logan.

Thankfully, the bucket of water did not dump on his head as planned but down the back of one leg. Surprisingly, I escaped unscathed ... until the next day when they both got their revenge and managed to pull the exact same prank on me, but with much more success. I graduated from high school and went on to Eastern Illinois University to earn a bachelor's degree in family services.

Dating-Marriage

I met Mark (my husband of thirty-nine years) my freshman year of college at the campus church I attended. There were over one hundred student members of the church, and on my first visit I must have met at least half of them, but Mark was the one I remembered. He was outgoing, friendly, and put me at ease, which is difficult to do. Unease sets in when I assume someone doesn't want to be around me. If I sense this at all, I'm gone. I will put the distance between us before the other person has a chance to. Mark and I went out on a date soon after our initial meeting. We played tennis with another couple and then went out for pizza. I don't think I said more than ten words the whole time. I'm surprised that he ever asked me out again, but he did. We went out casually over the next two and a half years and became really good friends.

During my junior year, we began dating exclusively. Mark took me for a walk at a park and asked me if I would be his girlfriend. This was a relief for me because I didn't know what to do with my ambivalence. If I thought that Mark was interested in me romantically, then I was interested in him, however, if I wasn't sure about how he felt, then I just considered him a really good friend, nothing more. I didn't dare take the risk of committing my heart or making my feelings known. I really needed him to do so first to reduce my chances of being rejected.

Our dating relationship went smoothly. I don't recall a single argument or even a minor disagreement. I know that is unrealistic, but at the time I didn't give it much thought. I figured we were meant for each other since we got along so well. I was easy to get along with. Acquiesce and everyone loves you.

There was one incident that could have been an argument but wasn't. I was just hurt. Mark had told my roommate and best friend that he was unsure about our relationship because I was not very expressive about my feelings towards him. He had even been wondering if we should keep dating. I think she was sworn to secrecy, but female friendship prevails in matters such as these. She told me about her conversation as soon as she walked in the door. I felt like the wind had been knocked out of me. On one hand, I was hurt that he had confided in my best friend before talking to me. It felt like a betrayal. On the other, I was breathless, frantic with thoughts that he was going to dump me, that he didn't want me. My mind was racing, wondering what I needed to do to keep from being abandoned by him.

A break-up is painful for anyone to endure, but for me it would have been more than painful; it would have been another stamp of disapproval, someone else saying, "You're not worth keeping."

The need to please is habit. If I behave the right way, do the right things, go along with the group, don't argue, act nice, and on and on, then my place is secure—whether in a family, friendship, or anywhere I am trying to belong.

I say "trying" because although I try, I don't often feel I belong anywhere. I had this incredible need to please Mark so I wouldn't lose him. Neither of us looked beneath the surface to understand why it was so difficult for me to express myself. We did know I needed to change in order to move our relationship forward. I'm still not very expressive even after thirty-nine years. I don't get overly excited about anything. It's safer to remain nonchalant because I'm less disappointed when things don't work out as planned. This is a point of contention at times in my marriage. I must have made some gains though. He proposed way back then, and we are still together today.

Mark is more expressive than I and will often probe for my reaction to a certain subject. Responses like, "Fine," "I don't know," and, "Okay," are reasonable answers (to me, with my dulled sense of personal awareness). Our wedding day was something I certainly looked forward to but did not get overly excited about. Inwardly, I was dancing, but outwardly I was calm and cool. This is not to say that I was not happy and thrilled to be marrying Mark, because I believe I was.

I simply did not want to get my hopes up or become too excited because I knew my happiness could all be taken away. Our early years of marriage went smoothly, just like our dating years. We had disagreements here and there, or I may have gotten my feelings hurt and sulked awhile, but there was never, ever a fight where we yelled or raised our voices at each other. I am a master at swallowing my emotions.

Children (Birthing Boys)

Are you old enough to remember the show *My Three Sons*? That's what I have— three wonderful sons— each unique in his own way.

My pregnancies were normal and healthy, except that I gained forty (or more) pounds with each of them. I always thought, as a mom, I was more suited for boys, so I was content. I grew up playing basketball, football, and whiffle ball. No dolls or "prissy" stuff for me. I was a tomboy in every sense of the word, and being called one didn't bother me. I could keep up with just about any other kid athletically (boy or girl) well into my junior high years, so the idea of teaching them how to swing a bat and throw a football was more appealing than having a tea party with stuffed animals. According to their play schemes, stuffed animals were for blowing up and having wars, not tea parties.

Birthing my children finally gave me a place to belong. They were mine, they came from me. They belonged to me, and I belonged to them. I finally knew what it meant to belong, to fit. Being a mother felt right.

The newborn idiosyncrasies didn't faze me one bit. I remember my first-born, Matthew, screaming while being given his first bath. I knew he was fine. I held him securely. I knew he would calm down once the bath was over, and he was swaddled in a blanket. Seeing my children sick was unnerving, though. Andrew had frequent ear infections and Jay battled asthma. Watching them suffer, I wished I could trade places with them. The boys are three years apart. Their births were greeted with anticipation and delight. I remember sitting, propped up against the nursery wall, belly protruding beyond its maximum limit, and daydreaming about holding the baby in my arms. I imagined him lying sound asleep in his crib.

The novelty didn't wear off after having our firstborn. With each pregnancy, I enjoyed getting out the baby clothes, arranging them neatly in the drawers, eagerly anticipating the day another baby would be rocking in my arms. Matthew must have been anticipating this arrival too. I came into his room one afternoon while he was taking a nap to find his belly protruding, just like mine. It was adorable. He had found a towel and stuffed it under his shirt to make it look like he was pregnant. Our third pregnancy was a surprise, and also a delight. Jay is our youngest son and I have told him he is the best surprise I have ever gotten or ever will get.

Birthdays, for me, were a quandary, a time of happy anticipation and serious emotions I never talked about. For as far back as I can remember, I have wondered if my mother was thinking about me. Did she know it was my birthday? Did she care? Has she forgotten me? I never verbalized these questions to anyone. After all, it was as if my life before adoption had been wiped clean. It didn't exist. I also remember always being dissatisfied, even when I got exactly what I wanted on my birthday. I was never complete. I suppose it was because the person who gave birth to me was not there to celebrate and affirm that my existence was a wonderful thing.

The first birthday party I remember was when I was in the third grade. It is memorable because I had long hair, and as I bent over to blow out my birthday candles, my hair caught on fire. I quickly put out the fire by clapping my hair between my hands. There was singed hair on the cake and the smell was horrible. We blew off the singed hair and ate the cake anyway. When I think back to the births of my children, I think of the following words: anticipation, excitement, joy, amazement, perfection, wonder, beauty, happiness, connection, peace, celebration. Even as they grow older, I look forward to celebrating birthdays with them. I worry that I fall short in making the days special for them. Whatever I do doesn't seem to be enough (to me).

I'm not sure I ever succeed in showing them how special they are. A few times in the last thirty-nine years, my birthday has slipped up on Mark. Once, he completely forgot. It was Saturday evening, and my birthday was the next day. He had not said a word about it. My initial plan was to let it go and not remind him. As I was vacuuming the floor and pondering the situation, I envisioned a few friends at church the next morning asking him about my birthday, or maybe even telling me, "Happy birthday!" I decided I'd better say something to him, I didn't want him to be humiliated. I turned off the vacuum as he entered the room and said, "I'm only telling you this because I don't want you to be embarrassed at church. Tomorrow is my birthday." He looked like he was facing an approaching tsunami with nowhere to run. Words came rushing at record speeds. "I was totally on top of it a month ago. I knew it was coming, I was thinking about it, about what to do." I listened as he peddled faster to escape the impending storm.

I'm not one to unleash lightning bolts of anger, so he got off easily. It cost him the price of a road bike I had my eye on—a nice road bike! I can think of only a couple of descriptors when it comes to my own birthday: regret and mistake. I don't like a big deal made about my birthday, and if (when) Mark forgets, then it just reinforces what I already fear: I'm not really worth keeping or remembering. My mind tells me this isn't true for me, nor would it be true for anyone else, but somewhere, deep inside, I struggle for validation.

Choosing to Stay at Home

I always wanted to be a stay-at-home mom. It was never really a question whether I would work outside the home or not. Leaving my children was never an option I even remotely considered. Maybe because that's exactly how I viewed it: *leaving* them, abandoning them.

The first time I left my oldest with a babysitter, he was about three months old. My previous employer was in a pinch and asked me to return for one day to fill in for someone who was ill. I reluctantly agreed. I left my son with a friend who had recently had a baby; she was only a five-minute drive from where I would be working for the day. It was the longest day of my life. I made a quick exit during the lunch hour, went to the sitter's home, and held my son. *I* was the one with separation anxiety! I remember picking him up at the end of the day, promising him (myself) that I would never do that again. Even now, twenty-five years later, as I write this, I am hit by a wave of emotions.

The resolve to never leave, never abandon is ever-present, but much deeper are these questions: *How could you leave me? How could you give me away?* My decision to stay at home is one I would make again. The choice has, however, had a direct impact on my sense of worthiness. I don't bring home a paycheck. I have nothing to put in the bank to show for my hard work and dedication. When asked, "What do you do?" I want to sneak out of the room. Being a stay-at-home mom doesn't seem to be "enough."

Financially, I could afford to stay at home because I also ran a home daycare. One summer I had five children in diapers. I needed a flow chart for diaper changes! It was exhausting work, but it enabled me to be with my own children.

I would make the same decision again today, but not working outside the home has affected me. When I think about my sons having children of their own, I think, *Please don't leave them.* This is not an indictment or judgment against women who work but merely a reflection of my own anxieties about abandonment.

One sunny afternoon, I was standing in the house watching two of my sons, then four and two years old. They played and romped around the living room. I was mesmerized. As I stood there, it dawned on me. *Four and two, that's how old my brother and I were when my mother gave us up for adoption.* My heart tore into pieces. I thought, *How could I ever hand them over to a stranger, never to see them again? How could I let someone else raise these two beautiful, wonderful boys who were a part of me? How do you do that? What would it do to them if I told them that they were going to have a new mommy and daddy? How could they possibly understand what was happening to them?* I wondered if it ripped her heart out.

At the time of this writing, my three sons live several states away in Georgia. It's especially disheartening right now because two of them are having birthdays this month, just nine days apart, and I'm not there to celebrate with them. I'm disconnected. The reality of my diminished role in their lives is hitting me hard, right between the eyes. It almost seems that they have replaced me with each other. On one hand, it's wonderful to know that they are good friends and enjoy hanging out together; on the other hand, I feel a bit displaced and kind of on the outside looking in.

Deciding to Adopt

Before we married, Mark and I talked briefly about adopting. The plan was to have two biological children and then adopt one. After we had our first two boys, the subject did not come up again. We were content with two children, so Mark planned to get a vasectomy. In between the "planning" and actual procedure, I got pregnant with our third child. Now with three children, adoption was out of the question. I felt that four children were too many for me. I enjoyed life with my three boys and did not miss having a girl.

Adding to my uncertainty about expanding our family through adoption was a conversation my mother had with Cathy, my younger sister by adoption. Cathy shared with her that she wanted to feel the closeness between mother and daughter that she witnessed in her friends. My mom explained the reason for this lack of closeness was that they weren't biologically related. When my mom relayed this conversation to me, my heart dropped. I knew if this was true for one adopted child in the family, it was true for all. Her statement was quite a blow. To hear from her lips that "biology" prevented a close connection between mother and child was devastating. My initial response was, "Well, you and dad aren't biologically related, and you feel a bond and deep love for him."

My mother called me the next day and apologized, saying that what she had said did not apply to me. I think the reality of it had already sunk in too deeply for an apology to wipe it away. What Cathy had done, which I was not yet in touch with, was expose an underlying rhythm of being and relating to one another without a deep, secure bond and attachment. It "worked" and was functional only on a superficial level. This bonding between mother and child is a delicate dance, and the dance takes two. The weight of this "responsibility" cannot solely rest on the adoptee; both mother and child must learn to "dance" together.

What I heard my mom saying was that she didn't feel a mother-daughter connection with me because I was not biologically hers. Naturally, my desire to adopt faded. I could not bring a child into my family only to have her feel "less than." I didn't want a child to feel that she wasn't enough, that she wasn't on an equal plane with any siblings.

Once we made the decision to adopt, Mark and I discussed little about these deeper issues, as most of our communication pertained to logistics: when to adopt, what country, finances, paperwork completion, etc. I don't remember talking about the challenges we would likely encounter or how adopting would affect our present family dynamic. Those were the days when I didn't deal with issues below the surface. That's one thing that has changed dramatically since adopting. Mark didn't share the few fears or concerns that I did express, probably because he didn't share my experience.

Looking back, maybe I was determined to prove that an adopted child could be loved as much as a biological one. And really, it's not about loving "as much." It's about the ability to "dance" together to form an attachment and a bond.

At the time, I think Mark held the belief that raising an adopted child was no different than raising a biological one. It isn't that you love them less, but you do arrive at that love differently. As the idea of adopting quickly became a reality, I was determined to be connected and bonded to this new addition, whoever she might be. I had an idealistic view that it would be easier for me and our adopted child to attach and form a bond simply because I understood what it was like to be adopted. Of course, understanding and love do not magically erase the wounds of another's own rejection and abandonment. Maybe I hoped that I could do for someone else what hadn't happened for me. I could not just find the dance floor. I could dance.

I felt compelled to give back, to give a child a home, but I was hesitant. I had a fierce love for each of my boys. Would I be able to have the same love for another child? I questioned and Mark quickly dismissed my doubts. He was confident that I had enough love in my heart for another child. It wasn't so much about having enough love, rather a fear that my love would not be enough. I didn't want our adopted child to feel like I had growing up—different, not loved in the same way as the biological child. That was the end of the discussion.

Friends and family members were adopting children during this time. Mark's brother and his wife began paperwork to adopt a little girl from China. I was thrilled for them and looked forward to the day we would meet their new daughter. We first met at Mark's parents' house. Shuang was an adorable two-year-old (exactly my age when I was placed for adoption); our birthdays are only two days apart. I sat back and quietly watched, imagining what she must be thinking as she was introduced to her new extended family. This can be such a confusing time for the adopted child, yet the adults are immersed in their own joy and admiration of this new family member.

A college friend who lived in Kansas also adopted a little girl from China soon after Shuang was adopted. Then, closer to home, good friends were awaiting their new son from India. We were following their process closely each step of the way. International adoptions are often one step forward and three steps back. We were thrilled and excited for them when they traveled to pick up their son. All this time, the thought never crossed my mind that adoption was in our future... until we attended the adoption celebration for their son.

The small celebration was followed by a short presentation from the director of their adoption agency. The director talked about the waiting children, specifically the plight of girls, who would never find a home. He said that many would end up on the streets of India as prostitutes. Mark and I simultaneously turned and looked at each other. No words were exchanged; we both knew what the other was thinking. We had so much. How could we not make room for another child, one who might otherwise end up living on the streets?

We went to a brief, informative meeting that afternoon with that same agency director. I don't remember a volley of discussion between Mark and me about the decision. Most likely, we would have come to the same decision, but hindsight tells me we would have benefited from a more thorough study of pros and cons of adopting a child into our family. We immediately began the long process.

Fortunately, Mark was in a slow period at his job, so he filled out most of the endless forms and paperwork. This was back when I still believed that I could not write. Even a simple questionnaire was daunting. Each Christmas, I asked him to write a letter to include in the Christmas cards. I had convinced myself that any letter I wrote would be no good. We would always go back and forth, with me always refusing, claiming ineptitude and Mark always countering with his own refusal but then caving when it became obvious that I wouldn't budge. Mark quickly made his way through form after form. Our home study was completed, dossier in order, and then came the long process of waiting. Month after month, we wondered about our daughter (we specified a female as our preference), hoped she was healthy, prayed she was well taken care of, and prayed that she would "fit" comfortably into our family. I now wonder if we adoptive parents realize what a tall order it is to ask a child from another culture or country to "fit" into our family, to be "grafted in" and not skip a beat, to really feel like they "belong." I wouldn't say that it's impossible, but I would say it can be a rather painful process with somewhat unrealistic expectations.

Adopting Maya

Adoption is a tangled mess of emotions. I feel guilty using the word "mess," but when you have conflicting emotions and feelings about something, the term "hot mess" applies. I should feel grateful that my parents adopted me when I needed a family, but I really didn't want a new family.

I see it this way. Imagine amputating a healthy leg and then giving that person a prosthetic limb and telling her she should be grateful. Then, you act surprised if she is not absolutely delighted with her new leg. What was wrong with the "leg" I had? My family was working just fine. There was nothing wrong with us (from my two-year-old point of view). The new family didn't feel like family at all. No matter how accustomed I got to the new family, they weren't my original members.

It's interesting that I chose a lifeless object to illustrate the adoptive family. I wonder if this is because a prosthesis cannot be mistaken for the real thing. My therapist likened it to an organ transplant. I like the organ transplant analogy. It makes complete sense, especially how both parts—the body and the transplanted organ—will feel the other doesn't belong. In a way though, it also hides the adoption issue. Of course, people who know your family will know of the transplant (adoption). This transplant, once it is "successful" (you get used to each other), becomes forgotten. The only visible signs are a scar (hidden under clothing) and anti-rejection drugs.

I wonder what anti-rejection drugs there might be for adoption. What can be done to reduce the risk of rejection on both sides? A prosthesis, too, can be hidden by clothing, and there may be no noticeable difference in one's gait. But clothing can also be removed at any time, and there is no denying that something is different, that your "leg" is a substitute for the real thing.

Adoption brings about a seesaw of feelings. I wanted adoption to be the same as birth relation, but they cannot be the same. If they were the same, there would be no pain, no rejection, no feelings of abandonment. If they were the same, your family of origin really wouldn't matter that much because they were replaceable. In other words, what I really think I am saying is, "I wish I had my family of origin."

Maya once told me (she was only six or seven at the time) she wished she had come from my tummy. I think she was saying she wanted to remain with the person who birthed her. She wanted the person she was raised by now, me, to be her "original" mother. She wished she had not lost that birth connection.

As much as adopting Maya was a joyful, (and at times stressful) experience, the above explanation of adoption applies to her as well. I'm sure she was quite happy with her family in India. She may not have had three meals a day, but she had a family, and to a child, that's what matters—a family who loves you. I don't expect her to feel "grateful" for being adopted. What a cruel burden to put on her. I also don't expect my sons to be "grateful" that I birthed them. What I expect is that she might feel incomplete. While I want her to feel accepted and part of the family, she may not always think that is the case. She may drift in and out of feeling like she belongs and fits in. My love for her is unconditional. I can love her completely even though there may be a part of her that cannot completely love me back. As an adoptee, I know that to love her father or me may sometimes feel like a betrayal toward her birth family. I get this and accept it.

One conversation with her actually deepened my desire to accept and love her, even if her love seemed incomplete. I reminded her that I wanted her to feel like she fit in, that she was like everyone else in the family, and that she was loved exactly the same. I explained that I knew what it was like to feel out of place. Her poignant and unexpected question almost took my breath away.

She asked, "Do you feel like you fit in (with your adoptive family) now?"

"No, I don't," I admitted.

"Well, if you don't feel like you fit in, how do you expect me to?" Her depth of emotion and insight cut a searing path through my heart. I was asking her to deny the truth. The truth is, she is *not* like everyone else in the family. Yes, her skin is dark brown, but more importantly, we are not her family of origin. Of course she is different. Of course she will *feel* different.

The truth is, I wish she could deny her loss. When she so fiercely faces her own grief and loss, I am forced to face my own. Adopting Maya put a mirror in front of me. Every day, I saw in that mirror a child who was

53

angry and hurt. I did not want to think about my emotions. Until I adopted a child of my own, who refused to let the anger be silenced, I was able to bury my feelings.

We met Maya on August 3, 2000, at O'Hare International Airport in Chicago. As we drove by the Chicago skyline, I felt like I was looking right through it. Someone made a comment about the famous "Serious" tower (the name given to the Sears Tower by Matt when he was about four years old). For me, the skyline was worlds away. Something odd was going on inside me. I felt the same way as we drove down the street to my birthmother's house for the first time. In both cases, maybe I didn't know how to comprehend such deep emotion. I was on my way to a huge, life-changing event; the world moved around me, but I was still, like I was underwater and hearing voices but not able to decipher what exactly was being said.

Fortunately, our case worker was able to escort Maya because she just happened to be visiting India and coming back to the states at the same time Maya was cleared for adoption. Maya's first experience with air travel was a nauseating one. She threw up often on the way to the states.

In the months leading up to that moment, I imagined what it would be like to meet my daughter at the arrival gate. Mostly, I considered her reactions and not mine. As we waited with family and friends, the anxiety and emotions welled up inside me. I wanted to find a private corner, sit down, and let the flood gates open. I knew better though. If I allowed even one tear to escape, there may be no end.

I worried I would relive what I had experienced when I was two and met my adoptive parents for the first time. I pushed it all back down inside, paced, walked, and distracted myself. I didn't want her first experience with me to be one in which I fell apart.

I envisioned the fairy-tale version of our initial meeting: Maya walking hand-in-hand with Shelby, our case worker, to the arrival gate to meet us. Really? Who was I kidding? She was carried by Shelby. Maya was wide-eyed with fear and suspicion. Shelby immediately handed her to me, all twenty-one pounds of her. She was so tiny yet almost five years old.

She didn't say a word or smile, she just looked from person to person with her beautiful brown eyes that asked, "What is going on?"

We sat in the arrival terminal for at least half an hour talking and admiring this precious little girl who had just left everything familiar to her. She now had a new family, language, and country, all in the matter of an airplane ride from India to the United States. We left the airport and went to our hotel for the night. Maya's hair had been cut, almost shaved, probably to get rid of lice. I bathed her in the tub. She squatted on her feet the entire bath, allowing me to pour warm water over her head. She didn't mind the water flowing over her face at all. She appeared to relish it. Her mood was serious. She took in all of her surroundings. After hours together, she still had not uttered a single word.

With jet lag and the time difference, I was prepared to be awake all night with her and didn't want the rest of the family to be awake as well. The boys and their dad took the bedroom. Maya and I slept on the sleeper sofa in the outer room of the suite. We put on our pajamas and slipped into bed. As I pulled up the sheet to cover us both, it went sailing over both of our heads. I saw her first smile and heard her first giggle. The moment was delightful.

I was awakened about 3:00 a.m. to the tiniest voice saying, "Paani peena hai." She wanted a drink of water. I was ready for the night shift, but she took a drink and went back to sleep until morning. That was her adjustment to the time zone difference. It couldn't have been any easier. Those first few days were quite magical. Everything was new to her. It was wonderful watching her enjoy the smallest things in life, like walking in grass. She was a little unsteady on her feet (we had yet to discover she has cerebral palsy), and always held her left arm bent and close to her chest. I don't think she had ever walked in grass before. She was barefoot and would step down in the grass and quickly raise her foot back up again.

I had my first ever tea party our first full day at home. She and I were both in pajamas, about ready to go to bed, but first, we sat in her room with the miniature porcelain tea set to have a tea party. As we pretended to enjoy our tea she began whining: "Biskut Khaana hai." She kept repeating it over and over. The words sounded so sad. I knew something must be wrong and had no idea what she was trying to communicate. Fortunately, I had met someone in the neighborhood who was from India. I called her and told her what Maya was saying. My neighbor translated the words: "Biscuit to eat." She was hungry. I didn't know how she could possibly be hungry. She had eaten more than I had at dinner that evening, but I was happy to bring her down to the kitchen for a bedtime snack.

Acclimating to brothers who liked to tease involved an ongoing game of them wearing blankets over their heads and slowly chasing Maya. She would squeal and run through the house screaming the universal children's mantra, "Mummy ko bolungi," translated, "I'm telling mommy!"

A couple of months after her arrival she was sitting on the floor playing with Legos when she articulated, in broken English, her yearnings for India. I was awash with sympathetic grief when I heard her emphatically proclaim, "America house, no more! India house!" My heart almost melted on the spot when I realized she missed India and everything familiar to her—the orphanage, her friends, her caretakers. I quickly ran up to her bedroom and brought down the mini photo album that had a few pictures of her time in India. We went through each one of them and talked about the people we saw in each picture. I told her I was so sorry she was missing her "India house." Even now it brings tears to my eyes.

Even though Maya has a family who dearly loves her, she lost the very thing that grounded her, that mattered, her family of origin … and life will never be the same. It might be easy to conclude that her life is better now that she has a family who can meet her needs. I would simply say her life is different. Sometimes, those differences are joyful. Sometimes, they are painful.

Missing Stories: Life Before the Age of Two

Sometimes, it feels like my life did not begin until I was two years old—until I was adopted. I think this is, in part, due to the silence surrounding my pre-adopted life and the existing paradigm of the time: "Children are resilient. Just give them a home and they will be fine. If they don't remember it, it won't matter- life goes on." I don't remember—maybe I should say, I have not been able to recall—the actual separation that took me away from my birth family; it matters greatly. It matters because the very foundation of my life was shaken, and not just shaken, but demolished, obliterated.

Everything I knew about family, love, security, and trust disappeared in a frightening car ride from Michigan to Indiana. To hold the notion that a family, regardless of how long one is in that family, is simply replaceable and in that sense doesn't "matter," is saying that to be true of any family, any relationship. If we can be replaced and never know the difference, then connection means little, if anything. My kids love to hear stories about when they were younger (what child doesn't?). It's fun to reminisce, telling all of the, "remember when," stories. For my youngest son, it was the story of how he would crawl across the carpeted floor with his head down, full speed, across the room. When he came up for air, he would have a rug-burn on his forehead. He did this more than once; the pain of the rug-burn did not seem to deter him. We tell the following story about my middle son.

One night while driving home with the family he started singing, in rapid succession, the lines to old classic songs. He sang for at least forty-five seconds. The songs just kept rolling off his tongue: "I found my thrill on blueberry hill, like a bridge over troubled waters, you ain't nothin' but a hound dog," and on and on. He had memorized one of those CD infomercials: "You can get all twelve CDs if you call within the next fifteen minutes."

When we realized he had memorized the commercial, we laughed so hard I thought my husband was going to drive off the road. My oldest loves to hear the story of how he jumped out of the car one evening, yelling about something magical in the sky. He was so excited and fascinated with what was "up there," he didn't think to look where he was running, which was directly into the light pole in the front yard. It stopped him dead in his tracks and flattened him to the ground. At least he had a perfect view of what had excited him.

One of the stories I tell my daughter is about how, when we first brought her home, she would not get off her bed in the mornings. After awakening, she would sit on her bed and call out "Mama?" (accent on the second syllable). She was almost five years old but sought approval for getting out of bed. It was endearing. Once I came in her room, she would happily crawl out of bed. There are many stories our children love to tell. One of the favorites is about Mark. One scorching summer day, temperatures were well into the nineties. We were at a Little League game for several hours where there were no bathroom facilities and no concession stand. One of the boys had to go to the bathroom, but it was a little too public to simply hide behind a tree. No problem. I had an empty McDonald's cup, complete with lid and straw (you know where this is going, don't you?), so he filled it up; he really had to go! We went back and watched the rest of the game. I completely forgot about the cup filled with urine getting warmer by the minute. An hour later we all came back to pile in the van and go home; we were all parched from the heat and lack of fluids. Mark was especially thirsty and noticed the McDonald's cup sitting in my cup-holder. It all happened so fast, and I was distracted by everyone getting in the van, so I didn't have time to react and stop him. He grabbed the drink while commenting on how thirsty he was and took a nice long swig through the straw. "Ah, what was that?!" He bolted out of the van spitting and sputtering. I didn't have to explain; he knew. Everyone else thought it was much funnier than he did.

Stories are important. The past is important, meaningful. Maya's life did not start at five years old, nor did mine start at two. I often ask her what she remembers about the orphanage. I want to keep her memories alive as much as possible. Keeping the memory of her birth family vivid is also important. At Christmas she hangs an Indian doll ornament on the tree as a reminder that she has another family. Each Mother's Day we buy flowers in memory of her mother. She picks out what she wants, and we bring them home and plant them. I believe it is as important for me as it is for her. It's my way of acknowledging to her that I am not her only mother. In fact, I am not her "original" mother. I am her second mother.

It's important for me to recognize this, accept it, and let her know so. I want Maya to feel safe keeping a special place in her heart for her birthmother without feeling like I am in competition with her. There is a "danger" in not acknowledging one's life before adoption. It forces all the questions and related feelings underground. It makes the birth family secret, off limits. The things that we normally keep hidden are shameful to us. I don't want the questions and feelings that arise from her past to be something she is ashamed of, but rather, something she can freely talk about and express—no matter what those questions and feelings are.

Not only do we recognize these special days, but very early on, probably when Maya was seven or eight years old, we talked about personalizing her mother. We looked at a list of several female Indian names and she picked one out for her birthmother. She picked out the name Rupali, which I think is absolutely lovely, and is indeed the name's meaning. Many people don't remember incidents that happened in their lives before the age of two, but others can (and should) tell them their stories of belonging. I did exist before the age of two but have no stories to fill in the gaps. I would like to know things like where I lived, who I lived with, and who watched me during the day. What was it like for my birthmother (and me) when she told us that we were getting a new mother and father? What made her wait four years before she put us up for adoption?

What exactly happened the day the man from the orphanage came and picked us up? Why wasn't my father in the picture? Did he ever lay eyes on me? All of these unanswered questions are missing puzzle pieces to my life story, and I need answers.

Layers

Layers. I need them in the wintertime. Not only in clothing, but layers of blankets while sleeping are a must. As I write this, I'm tempted to take a break and go walk a labyrinth. I guess that's about layers too, in a geometric kind of way. I'm thinking more about emotional layers though, specifically the ones I relied on in my younger years to survive the trauma of abandonment and adoption. I believe that, initially, being adopted was traumatic, even though I don't remember the feelings or events of my relinquishment, time in the orphanage, or being taken away by the strangers who were to adopt me. What I do remember is talking myself into feelings of acceptance and gratitude. During my grade school years and through most of high school, my attitude toward my adoption was that it was: the best thing for me, God's plan, meant to be, a good thing, and wonderful (that may be a stretch, but I thought that way).

The safest place to dwell was on the surface layer of denial. I told myself that I was not interested in ever knowing who my birthmother was. If she didn't want me, then I didn't want her. I cloaked myself in denial, pretense, and stoicism. Recently a young adoptee told me that she felt her adoption was "pretty special." Yes, I think I might have felt that way at one time. Maybe that's one of the layers, but it seems like a thin one that can easily be shattered, one you could fall through and drown. My heart sank when this young adoptee told me she felt "pretty special." Inside, I said, *No, it's a lie. Adoption is not special at all.* How can you truly feel "special" knowing someone didn't want you? What is special about that?

I liken adoption to buying off the seconds rack at the clothing store. The rejected, less-than-perfect get sold for less. This layer in particular, is quite difficult to come to terms with. I can't hide from it either. It's everywhere.

Not only do my own adoption issues stare at me in the mirror every morning, but also the issues of the innocent girl walking down the hall from her room. Issues are at my back door (my neighbor and good friend has two adopted children), and everywhere in my family (adopted siblings, a daughter-in-law, niece, and sister-in-law).

I am sometimes approached by friends for "help." One recently told me of a coworker who has taken in her two-year-old nephew. His mother died, and the father is uninvolved. This surrogate mother is having a rough time with her distraught nephew and her own misgivings about having to take care of him. My friend asked if I would talk with her coworker and offer her what support I could. "Sure," I said, even though I don't have a grasp of it myself. My heart goes out to this poor little guy and his aunt, who, without support, is not going to be able to give him what he needs. What is so sad is that what he really needs, he can never get back.

Thus, I feel that all of these layers of adoption are screaming at me from all directions, and I cannot even grasp one, sit with it, let it be just as it is, and be okay.

Mine may be a wound that never heals. I wonder if my efforts are wasted. Is healing even possible? I am told that it is. I stare into a glowing fire as I think about these layers, wondering how to get to the innermost core of these emotions.

Digging diamonds would be much simpler, and I imagine I would have many willing participants to help. Instead, I'm digging up a partially decayed corpse, and who wants to be anywhere near that? No one! The stench of buried guilt, shame, regret, anger, fear, and loss are toxic, or at least it appears that way to me. Somehow, unearthing the layers, getting them out of the shadows, must be healing. I often feel that my efforts to heal actually open a never-healing wound.

Part of the struggle in this excavation is feeling responsible for wounding others. When I ask questions, I communicate that "I'm not satisfied, something is missing, and what you did is not enough." This, I believe, is what others hear, but not necessarily what I am saying. I need to know, to fill in the blanks. I need to find those missing puzzle pieces and complete the picture.

My digging forces others to face some of their own skeletons, many of which, I believe, they would rather leave buried. If I will just keep quiet and remain on the outer layer of denial, then everyone (but me) is happy. Life goes on. Digging means possibly ending up at the core of where everything initially started. There lies the possibility of being rejected—again—and who would want to relive that suffering?

Peeling these layers away, slowly, one at a time, is precisely what I must do to find my authentic self—the core of who I am. Those who have known me for some time would probably characterize me as reticent, loyal, compliant, reliable, easy-going, and patient. While I may possess all of those qualities, there are many more, both light and dark, below the surface.

Maya just passed on to me something she recently read about how great light casts great shadows. There is a balancing to all the wonderful, positive qualities we hold. The shadow, the darker side (like anger) is safer to keep hidden. Keeping these shadows buried makes me one-dimensional and makes day-to-day life numb, but helps me maintain an even keel. That also ensures there are few valleys and even few mountain tops.

Neglecting the task of peeling away the layers also promotes secrecy. I finally mustered the courage to begin asking questions about my suspicions of abuse and an amazing thing happened for someone else. I asked my birthmother if she was aware of any abuse during the two years she parented me. She was not aware of any and remarked that her father would have never let something like that go unresolved. What the question did for her was bring back memories of abuse she suffered at the hands of a family friend and member of her church.

The memory was locked away, never disclosed to anyone. She had "forgotten" about it (which is a "safe" thing to do with unpleasant memories). She was able to recall it and talk to her husband about the abuse. My digging and peeling away at the layers brought about some healing for her.

It makes me wonder what carrying that memory all those years, never telling a soul, has done to her physically and emotionally. I'm glad, for her sake, that it finally came out.

Pretending Layer

It's wonderful to watch children lost in a make-believe world, like the princess enjoying a tea party with stuffed animals. With three boys, I often watched all-day superhero dramas. My favorite costume of all time (which I made one year for Halloween), is Spider-Man. All three boys lived in the costume, which I saved. The brilliant blue body suit is set off by a red breastplate adorned with the spidery silver webbing made of fabric paint. I created two masks so both boys could be Spider-Man at the same time. This was genius forethought on my part, saving me from refereeing the assured battles that would have erupted over one mask.

We outgrow the fairy-tale and superhero play, but we don't leave pretending behind. The habit stays with us. I pretended for years. Occasionally, the need arose to fight off and push down realities as they attempted to surface. I pretended that I was comfortable with my own adoption, that it didn't bother me, it didn't matter, I fit in, I was even "happy" about it and better off. I may have carried this on forever had I not adopted a little girl who refused to "pretend." She was angry, in turmoil over her lost family of origin, and honest. Pretending leads to silence and no ongoing communication about ambivalent feelings. The act is dangerous and produces a false self that others come to accept as the "real" self.

Guilt Layer

At two years old (like every other two-year-old) my entire universe was my family. Nothing else mattered except that my family would be there each morning when the sun came up. When I was passed along to strangers, I must have come to the conclusion that I had done something wrong. Why else would I be sent away? Naturally, guilt followed shame. This is when the tentacles grew and began to branch out.

I internalized guilt as a habitual thought. *What else is there to feel guilty for?* My answer was a host of things: asking questions, wishing things had been different, not feeling connected, bringing up uncomfortable issues, searching for my birthmother and birthfather, not keeping quiet, ambivalence, writing a book about all the above, etc.

Fear Layer

Fear attaches its tentacles to several other layers. The most profound and gripping fear is that of being rejected all over again. Fear breeds secrecy, silence, fake behavior, distrust, and stoicism. Fear leads to building walls of protection.

In *The Book of Awakening*, Nepo writes about counting by touching, not adding or subtracting. He tells a story about awakening after surgery with a friend at the foot of his bed whose gaze was elsewhere. He writes: "I knew in that instant she was already mourning me, and so she missed me coming alive. She was already preparing for the life without me, and so, the deeper closeness awaiting us was never felt or worn." Fear can do that to you, lead you to mourn what might happen, and you miss the connections, intimacy, and closeness that comes with embracing each moment and simply allowing events to unfold. You miss life.

I remember many nights trying to drift off to sleep with the fear of something horrible happening to my adoptive parents. I mourned their deaths, fearing that they, like my birth parents, would not be permanent in my life. It's nearly impossible to allow life to unfold with this underlying fear as your base mindset.

As children, our fears are often unfounded and results in misunderstandings. While camping one summer with my aunt and uncle, I was convinced that a snake was lying coiled in the corner of my tent, only a few feet from my sleeping bag. I lay awake, fighting off sleep, fearing the snake would slither my way during the night. I woke the next morning to find that I was afraid of a tent cover, that, in the shadows, looked like a coiled reptile.

The fear of being rejected is real for me. It happened once. It could happen again. I have (unknowingly) sought protection and reassurance that the people in my life are solid, not going anywhere, and here for the long haul. I need to know that they are not just present in body, but also in spirit, and that they are permanently connected and emotionally engaged.

Anger Layer

Anger must be near the core. I don't believe I have gotten that far. I see glimpses but have yet to feel its fury. It's so much easier to see another's anger than my own. I see Maya's anger on a weekly basis. She does not hide it or pretend that she doesn't feel it, which is refreshing. I see the beauty in her anger and rage. Yes, beauty. The rage says, "I am worth keeping. I have intrinsic value. I am a beautiful being." Her anger does not scare me or cause me to retreat. I simply let it be and allow her to vent.

Allowing Maya to express her full range of emotions validates her. By doing so, I am saying, "I'm sorry you have to bear that wound." Exhausted, I sometimes wonder if there will ever be an end.

This is an important point to ponder. If *I* venture down the path of anger as Maya does and allow myself to be engulfed by its turbulence and passion, will there be an end? Do I even have a right to be angry? Some would argue that I do not. Who am I to argue or protest against what "God has done" in my life?

I believe that God can work with whatever mess we make, but he does not "make" our messes. I am blessed with a faithful husband and four wonderful children, so why should I be angry at all? Is there another life I would rather have? Maybe there is no anger. Or maybe it lies beneath those layers of pretense, fear, stoicism, silence, numbness, distrust, worthlessness, shame, and guilt.

Why I Searched

I had always told myself, while growing up, that I didn't want to know who my birthmother was. If she didn't want me, then I didn't want to know her. Of course, I would fantasize about who she was: she had lots of money and was a prominent, important, and influential woman. I remember only one occasion when I approached the subject of my birthmother with my mom. I was in the sixth or seventh grade and had a dream about being at a party where someone told me my birthmother's name. I awoke just as the person told me, but for the life of me, I couldn't remember the name she spoke.

Casually, I began telling my mom about the strange dream. Everything was strikingly vivid about the dream, except for my birthmother's name; I just couldn't recall it. My mom responded, "Ooh, I know her name."

"You do?" I asked.

She said, "Yes, would you like to know it?"

I replied nonchalantly, "Sure."

She told me her first and last name, and I think all I said was, "Oh." Then I went directly to my room and wrote it down in the back of my Bible. We never spoke about it again, but I never forgot her name.

So, even though I told myself that I never wanted to know her, I believe that down deep in my soul, I desperately wanted to know. It was easier and safer to deny my desire than accept and feel the pain of rejection, of not being wanted. As an adult, when the thought of searching came up, I always pushed it aside out of fear that searching for my birth family would hurt my parents' feelings. I just couldn't do that to them. It would appear ungrateful on my part for all they had done for me.

When I finally acted upon my desire to search, I was thirty-three years old with three boys of my own. I had just finished a phone conversation with my mom about borrowing their camper for a trip. I had heard my sister (the only biological daughter of my parents) mention that they had borrowed it to go camping, so I was sure it wouldn't be a problem for our family to do the same thing.

Much to my shock, hurt, and disappointment, it was a problem. My parents felt that for insurance reasons my borrowing the camper wasn't a good idea. As soon as I hung up the phone, I decided to start searching for my birthmother. No longer could I deny my desire just because it might hurt someone else's feelings. What that one phone conversation did was solidify what I had always felt growing up. I wasn't REALLY one of the family.

They felt differently about me. I wasn't their biological child, so they didn't love, didn't connect, and didn't bond with me the same way they did with their own child. This was my perception; I cannot say what my adoptive parents feel in their hearts. I suppose that even if they felt absolutely no difference between their biological child and me and treated us equally in every way, I still would doubt and wonder if they could accept and love me the same. After all, my own

74

birthmother didn't want me, so why would someone not even related to me want me?

I didn't tell my parents I was searching; it was later, after I found my birthmother, that I finally told them what I had done. Even as I type that phrase, "what I had done," I imply that I did something wrong and had to fess up to my adoptive parents.

I say very little about my birthmother in the presence of my adoptive parents. I don't offer any information unless they ask for it. Even then, the details are minimal. I sense their unease with the whole issue, and so, to protect their feelings, I keep quiet.

Searching For My Mother

Surprisingly, it took only about two and a half weeks to find my mother. The orphanage I was sent to was affiliated with a nondenominational church. I had every reason to believe that my birthmother and her parents were members of the same church. I started calling the churches near where I was born in Michigan who also supported the orphanage. I told them I was looking for some family members and asked if the Ferguson family were members of their church. Each person I talked to said no but gave me another number to try. After the fourth contact number, I had located the church where my family had been members. I was given another name and number to call. I didn't know it at the time, but I was calling my cousin. When she picked up the phone, I gave her my name, told her I was looking for a family member, and asked her if she knew Edith Ferguson.

"You're looking for Edith?" she asked with familiarity in her voice.

At this point my mind raced for what to say next. I tried to gently tiptoe. I had no idea if my inquiries would be seen as intrusive. I continued, "Yes, I'm not sure how to explain this, but—"

She interrupted, and the words came out slowly. "Are you her daughter?"

With relief, I said, "Yes."

Then she gasped, "I used to babysit you."

At this point, I shook inside and out. This was the first steppingstone, and I had a long way to go before actually knowing if I would ever meet my mother. I told my cousin that I had no idea if my mother was interested in talking with and meeting me, but I was interested in meeting her. She said she would make a call to her mother (my aunt) and get in touch with Edith that way.

I gave her all my contact information and waited, not knowing if I would ever hear from my mother. Days passed. Nothing. Each time I returned home after being away, even if only for a short time, I immediately checked the answering machine. Several weeks passed.

Then she called. I remember sitting on my bed and talking to her, but I don't remember much of the conversation. In that initial phone conversation, we talked about meeting. The decision was quick.

· Our family decided to make the long drive from Illinois to Texas to meet her and her husband just a couple months later. After two long days on interstates, we made it to Texas. I still remember pulling up in their driveway in our big blue conversion van. Feelings and emotions were driving inward like water going down a drain. I felt numb but apprehensive. It was safer just not to feel anything.

I stepped out of the van as she came out to meet me. I don't know what it was like for her, but for me it was like meeting a complete stranger. She could have been anyone I passed on the sidewalk or in the grocery store on any given day. If I sound callous, know that I don't mean to be. I just did not feel a bond or connection. I did not have the feeling you might have while enjoying an embrace with a long-lost friend.

I felt distant, detached, wary, and I wasn't surprised these were the prevalent emotions. Having Mark present for that first meeting was a lifesaver. He carried the conversation for most of the visit. I showed her my photo book that chronicled my years from kindergarten through high school. She appeared, to me, uninterested. Maybe it was too painful for her to look at the years she had missed, or maybe my perception was skewed. There was so much silence surrounding the whole issue.

As time passed, I asked more questions, and she became more silent. That first meeting was seventeen years ago. Today, I still feel no real connection. In part, I attribute this to her lack of vulnerability. She is reluctant, even now, to answer questions I have about my relinquishment. Actually, she has been more than reluctant; she simply doesn't respond to my emails that contain questions about that time in our life.

I believe the only chance for a connection with her is to shine a light on the details, good and bad, of my relinquishment. From where I stand, there can be no connection without full disclosure. The level of connectedness is directly proportionate to the level of disclosure.

Meeting Her for the First Time

In the seventeen years of "knowing" my birthmother, we have been together only six times. Each time we have been together, the encounter bears increasing anxiety on my part, which is different from the first time we met.

I think I experienced that first meeting in Texas in a detached and dissociative manner. As we drove down the street to her house on that sweltering day in August, my husband asked, "How are you feeling?"

I really could not afford to "feel" anything at that moment, and I said, "Fine." I remember greeting her as I stepped out of our van and thinking there must be some familiarity on her part. The last time she saw me, I was two years old, but I was her daughter. I had no recollection, much less a last memory, of her.

For some strange reason, I did not put much thought into the initial meeting in the days leading up to it. I just thought, *We are going, we will meet, and we will stay with her for four or five days.* All other ideas and emotions were kept at bay. Each evening, when I could retire to my room, I felt relieved, not because my mother was a difficult person (she is a wonderful individual), but because I didn't have to be "on."

It's difficult to experience a moment of this magnitude but talk around the issues that created said magnitude. The only discussion we had about her decision to place my brother and me for adoption was a brief moment during a car ride to dinner. We were sitting next to each other, and my mother said that giving me up was the best thing for everyone. She wouldn't have the life she had now, nor would I.

I numbly nodded my head in agreement. We stayed at her house for about five days, but I remember so little. Why? We took the boys fishing, and I remember spreading a blanket on the grass and giving my youngest a bottle of juice. I put a worm on my fishing hook for the very first time in my life. My mother loves fishing. I hate touching slimy worms, but I was not about to play the helpless, squeamish female who can't bait her own hook. I hated every moment of it, but I did it.

I suspect the issues surrounding my relinquishment are painful and shame-inducing for my birthmother. Her silence makes her fragile in my eyes; I'm afraid I will break her by asking too many or the wrong questions. I am reluctant and careful not to overstep my bounds. I'm not even sure where my boundaries begin and end in this whole thing. I wonder if I have the right to ask questions, to unearth what she seems to have buried.

During that first visit, Walt (Edith's husband) told Mark that he could always tell when Edith was depressed and thinking about my brother and me. He would notice her countenance and say, "You've been thinking about those kids again, haven't you?" The effects of the relinquishment stayed with her, just like they did me. Fifteen years later, we met again. It was the summer of 2010.

To reflect on my birth mother's visit in 2010, I have to rewind the three days in my mind and simply be a spectator. In my replay, what I first notice is that no one in my family is deeply connected to her, which is not surprising, given the little time that we've spent together over the last seventeen years.

How should each person feel? Like family, distant relatives, friends, mere acquaintances? The initial interactions feel forced. How do you receive someone who is related when the relationship is awkward and distant? It's like meeting a stranger for the first time, every time.

In my memories, I see myself looking her over (hopefully without her noticing). Most children probably don't think twice about looking like their parents or having some of the same mannerisms. They have surely heard more than once how much they resemble one or both of their parents. I never heard this growing up, so now, as I look at her, I wonder if we look alike. Will I look like her in twenty years, do we walk the same, talk the same, have any of the same quirks or habits?

I think I catch her doing exactly the same thing. Maybe she's wondering, *Is she really my daughter?* The thought certainly crossed my mind, *Is this woman really my birth mother?* It is so strange to sit across the table from a stranger who gave birth to you.

I know that Edith likes to bowl and quilt, she belongs to the Methodist church, and she volunteers with a mentoring program. I know little about who she is on the inside. She is well-guarded. I'm the one who should be guarded when around her. She is the one who hurt me, but she acts like she is hurt. We talk of nothing significant, which feels like a waste of time to me. Why come all that way to talk about nothing? No matter how often I rewind and replay those three days, I learn nothing.

Mark made a remark about Edith finding a great guy in Walt. He said Walt is the kind of guy who would have pursued her even if she did have two small children. Of course, she didn't have children when they met because she sent us to an orphanage. When Mark said that, I had never thought about how Walt might have married her even if she had kept us, and I would know him today as my father. I think he'd be a great dad. She could have had at it all—her kids and the man she fell in love with.

Mark left for a business trip midway through their visit. My anxiety magnified. I tried to fill up the time with activities. With too much empty time, I could blurt out something regretful.

My feelings toward Edith have been changing (not specifically toward her but about the whole situation). Initially, my feelings mirrored my childhood thoughts about adoption: it was the best thing, it was meant to be, I'm fine with it, even glad about it, it doesn't bother me, I completely understand and accept it. She did the best thing, right thing, what she had to do, I'm fine with her decision, it's okay, etc.

Being okay with her decision is hard, yet I feel like accepting her decision is necessary. What's done is done. If she had kept us, I may have lived out my teenage years just like her. I may have repeated her mistakes and been a wild teenager, single and alone with two small children.

I guess I should be grateful that things turned out the way they did. I want the best of both worlds. I want my life but without being dumped as a two-year-old.

Belonging

I remember being in stores and passing women old enough to be my mother and wondering what she looked like. I wondered if it was possible that I could pass her on the street, open a door for her, or sit next to her in a cafe and never know it. This was not likely, but it was possible. Any woman I ever encountered could be my birthmother, and I would never know it. What a strange concept. I looked into the eyes of strangers and searched for my mother, my identity, me.

I looked for belonging, but I no longer feel that need. I once was hers, but I'm not anymore. Sadly, I can't say that I actually feel like I belong in my adoptive family either. I was grafted in. I'm a prosthetic.

In the fifth grade, I tried for the first time to connect with my family of origin, although the details are a little fuzzy. It was Christmas time, and we had gathered with my dad's side of the family to celebrate and have a gift exchange.

That year I only put one gift on my list: a Detroit Lions football jersey. We lived in Illinois, and my dad was a Chicago Bears fan, but I wanted a Lions jersey. I had planned how to respond if anyone asked me why I preferred the Lions over the Bears. My line was, "I like the color of the Lions' jersey." In actuality, it was a way for me to connect with my family of origin. I was born in Trenton, Michigan, just south of Detroit. I was making a statement, if only to myself. *These are my roots. Michigan is where I belong.*

Maya and I had a particularly poignant conversation one afternoon. She shared fears, one of which was being left again. She said she feared that Mark and I would not pick her up from camp. She was flying alone to visit (in the U.S.A.) her friends from the orphanage and worried that when she got off the return flight, we wouldn't be there waiting for her. She also had fears of us sending her to live with another family.

She then asked me if I had ever felt this way. I couldn't remember the fear of being sent away to live with another family, but I told her that I remember feeling like my parents didn't love me the same as their biological child and that I didn't really belong or fit in. I stressed that I didn't want her to feel that way. I told her I wanted her to feel completely loved and accepted because she is.

We had just started therapy for Maya, but I joined her because she refused to go alone. This conversation is the one that opened my eyes to my own need for therapy. I had never talked about the issues that she fearlessly shared in the open. I had buried them so deep that my daughter's struggles forced them to the surface. I was crushed to think that I cannot make Maya feel like she belongs, and I worried that she may *always* feel as if she does not belong.

"Adopted" Into Therapy

Maya needed therapy. I didn't. I wasn't looking for a therapist. I had, after all, been able to "manage" my adoption issues. I had come to terms with my relinquishment and adoption while very young; I was completely fine with it, or so I had convinced myself. Maya, on the other hand, was full of rage. The fact that I always kept my cool, even when she was angry, only added fuel to her fire. It infuriated her that I did not mirror her anger. It was almost as if she was saying, "Please tell me that I am not alone in my anger. You are angry too, right?"

I now understand her need to have a comrade. I have met very few adoptees who do not have ambivalent feelings about adoption. It could be that the few who don't disclose these feelings are in denial or unaware of the territory waiting to be explored. On the rare occasion that an adoptee tells me he/she never thinks about it, or has no negative feelings at all, I, like Maya, want to say, "You have these mixed feelings too, and you just can't talk about it or admit it, right?"

I, like Maya, needed a comrade. Maya found, in me, someone who "gets it," which can be a blessing and a curse. The blessing is being understood. The curse is opening a path to deep wounds and pain. Denial is easier when you don't have a daughter who is also a mirror.

When the wounds are validated, especially by someone who has felt/feels the same way, they become more real. I never, ever, would have considered therapy (I didn't need it, right?) had it not been for Maya. I had tunnel vision. "I'm fine. I'm fine. I'm fine." Maya, by her expressiveness, her outward display of anger regarding her history, led me out of the tunnel to an awaiting vista of emotions. I believe I always knew there were conflicting feelings inside, but I never wanted to think about it long enough to let them surface.

Some of the views are the muddy, murky, alligator-infested marshes, but some are breathtaking views of snow-capped mountains. There is a rare beauty in forming a family by adoption. It is, at least for now, for me, more beautiful from the adoptive parent's perspective than that of the adopted child or adult adoptee.

If the people in my life had been more aware of the complicated side of adoption from the adoptee's perspective, and had they accepted the myriad of emotions, I might have been better able to see that beauty.

If others had accepted the complicated feelings, I would have had permission to feel them and maybe heal them. Maya deals with her ambivalent feelings with gale force winds, which can be endlessly draining. I would have it no other way. I would rather know, and want her to know, exactly what she is feeling.

At first, I thought Mark and I had made a mistake by taking her to a therapist. From my perspective, we were opening up wounds that could never be healed. After spending a few sessions with her, I learned my wounds were unhealed. It seemed cruel to make her

87

feel the pain and anger of something that could never be "fixed."

Now, I think feeling leads to healing. Maya is well on her way to healing. I believe she feels things deeply and often openly. I, on the other hand, lean on numbness and thus stall my progress. Over four decades of sequestered emotions finding their way to freedom is like a swarm of bats escaping from their dark cave at night, except with a twist. Years of keeping things inside has narrowed the route of escape, so these little "beasts" are erupting through a pinhole.

Touching these wounds is necessary. For so long, I had a hands-off approach, much like a child who protects a new scrape or laceration from anyone's touch—it's much too painful. If untouched, the wound won't hurt. But, if untouched, the wound may not heal.

How do you go about touching the wounds of adoption? How do you begin to feel what you have always told yourself doesn't hurt and doesn't matter? Our fortuitous decision to adopt was, ironically, the beginning of touching these wounds. The wheels were set in motion. All those months of waiting, thinking, contemplating what it would be like to finally see our daughter, began to awaken the comatose emotions of my own relinquishment.

At the time, I thought my emotionality was related only to Maya and longing for her to be with us, impatiently waiting for her to finally be united with her new family. I daydreamed about what she might be doing, wondered if she had enough to eat and if her needs were being met. I almost always ended up teary eyed and wishing I could hop on a plane, bring her home, and put an end to the waiting.

I will be forever grateful that Maya's journey here to our family led me to my pilgrimage of sorts. Three years ago I embarked on a pilgrimage across Spain. I walked the Camino de Santiago. It took me a month. I carried everything I needed on my back. It's amazing how little we really need. At the time, I didn't know all the reasons that compelled me to begin the journey. I just knew I wanted/needed to do it. Therapy has been a similar experience, with the clarity of why I need it coming into clearer focus as I move through the process.

Asking Questions: Putting the Puzzle Pieces Together

I had just settled in to do some writing when Maya came down the stairs looking for me. When she saw that I was busy, she said, "Oh, never mind." I asked her what she needed, and she said she wanted help writing a letter to a couple from church about their plans to adopt a baby. Her voice trembled as she said, "That's okay. You're busy." I was tempted to let her go back up the stairs, but her quivering voice told me that she needed support. I asked her what she wanted to say in the letter, and she started crying. She explained that she didn't know why she was crying.

I pressed her for more information. She wanted to tell the family that adoption wasn't all happy and wonderful and that there is a sad side to it as well. I remember her asking through the sobs, "Why is adoption so difficult?" I told her it's difficult because there is a part of her that has been lost that can never be replaced. Everything isn't "fixed" and wonderful just because she has another family now. I sensed that she needed affection. I asked her if she wanted to sit with me in the rocker. She needed no coaxing and plopped into my lap, commenting that she was too big. Then she covered herself with a blanket, curled up, and let the tears roll.

She asked again about her story, particularly about why her parents didn't keep her. I have to speculate since I don't have all the facts, but my best guess is that she was so ill, her parents took her to the hospital for fear that she would die if she didn't receive medical attention. She still has not asked why they never came back for her. As I look back, I feel that I should have been more nurturing, affectionate, and comforting. I should have given her more, and yet, a part of me is amazed that I was able to give her anything at all.

The non-stop emotional support given is draining because it surfaces the realization that no such support and understanding was offered to me while growing up. While I'm grateful to lend this support and understanding, it also rubs an unhealed wound inside.

Adoption talk comes up almost on a weekly basis.

I give her so much support, while no support was given to me—most likely because I didn't ask questions; I kept everything inside. This may be because it was not something we openly discussed from the beginning of my life with my adoptive family.

I recently began more boldly asking my adoptive parents more questions. I wrote my mother and asked her what life was like those first few months.

She wrote, "I'm trying to put myself in your shoes today. I continue to wonder why [you ask] this question. I'm sure you must feel a void of some kind that perhaps this will fill."

Yes, a void. This is not a reflection on my adoptive parents, but the result of an invasive interruption in my life. What I hear beneath the statement, "You must feel a void of some kind," is, "You have a family now. You should not have a void to fill. It's not okay to ask questions; why does it matter after all these years? It's in the past, over and done."

If my adoptive mother literally answered the way I interpret, I might be crushed beneath the emotional weight of such ignorance, and I don't mean stupidity. Simply put, there is a lack of knowledge and understanding of the intricacies of adoption.

I imagine what relief and freedom I would feel if she answered, with deep sincerity, "Please tell me, Terri, because your feelings matter deeply. Help me understand so that I can reassure you."

Asking questions feels like a betrayal. Wanting to know about my history, my biological family, feels like a betrayal. I feel like I'm saying to my adoptive family, "You're not enough." It really is not about whether or not they are "enough." If I ask too many questions and offend them, it could lead to more rejection and another abandonment. This puts me in an impossible situation—

I want to know but feel I can't ask. I must be the one who protects everyone else's feelings, but I am the victim. I, the child, am responsible for making sure this whole adoption thing "works out."

In July of 2010, Maya asked me to read a poem she wrote. The verses began, "This is it, this is me, are you ashamed of what you see, or of what you see in me that you don't get? Are you ashamed of me being me?"

I told her it was really deep.

She said, "I don't really think about it. I just start writing."

I read the verses as, "Do you like me, will you accept me, even the part of me that you don't yet understand? I act one way, but it really means something entirely different. I don't even 'get' myself sometimes, so how could you possibly understand me? I am who I am. Is that okay, questions and all? I cannot change who I am, so I hope you will accept me. Maybe then, I can accept myself without apology."

My response to Maya was, "Be who you truly are, run free with no unhealthy ties to another and not shackled by opinion. Another person's choice does not define you. Be who you truly are, a rare beauty full of grace, loyal and kindhearted, gifted in what really matters."

I welcome Maya's questions. I wish she would ask more of them, even though they are sometimes hard to hear and hard to answer. I especially worry when she questions her self-worth. Her continual questions about self-worth unearth my own. When she makes comments about not being "good" at anything, I think she has an insatiable need to hear me tell her all the things she does well. Oddly, when I tell her, she argues with me. Sometimes I just want to say, "Would you just believe how wonderful you are, please?"

Looking in the mirror

Have you ever held up a mirror at just the right angle to get the infinity reflection? You see yourself holding the mirror about ten times; it just goes on and on. That's kind of what's going on with my neighbor, Kelly.

The light tapping of footsteps coming up the steps to the deck and back door brought a smile to my face as my neighbor Kelly and her son Kyle came bearing unexpected but wonderfully aromatic gifts. The smells of grilled chicken, roasted vegetables, and rice initiated a rumbling in my stomach. The delight of not having to fix my own dinner quickly turned to a sinking feeling as I saw the exhausted and hopeless look on Kelly's face.

"Our dinner plans have changed; our fifteen guests won't be joining us now. I didn't want all this food to go to waste." Our eyes meet, hers trying to say it all without saying anything in Kyle's presence, mine trying to read between the lines. I wasn't catching on and assumed it had something to do with work. Her son was with her but went home. She stayed and began to cry. Then she opened up about canceling the dinner. She said she had, "had enough."

She has two adopted children. They were young at the time, and she had reached another breaking point. I wanted to tell her that life would get better, they would adjust, their behavior wasn't their fault, etc. She knew all this, but such knowledge is useless when dealing with the day-to-day struggles of parenting.

I wanted to tell her something to make her feel better and give her a way to fix the problem. I wanted to tell her, "I'm sorry [we adoptees] can sometimes be difficult children, but please, don't give up on us."

The most difficult part is being in both sets of shoes. I know what it feels like to be the parent ready to throw in the towel and what it's like to be the adopted child. I have such compassion for her two kids; it's much easier to muster this compassion and understanding when it's not your own child.

Here is my take on something that occurs with some adopted children. Physically, there is something called proprioception (knowing where your body is in space). With my eyes closed, I can touch my nose even though I can't see it. You have a good sense of your body and where its parts are in relation to the whole, without even having to consciously think about it. Everything fits together, and you know where it all fits. You can feel every part. When I close my eyes and think about my knees, I can physically feel where they are, even without reaching out and touching them. How incredible is that?

Emotionally speaking, proprioceptive qualities are missing for many adoptees. We don't know where we belong or if we belong at all. When I'm with my adoptive family, I don't really fit; after all, I'm not physically theirs. I don't fit with my biological family either. I haven't been with them for decades. Neither group feels right. There is nothing internal that says, "This is where you belong."

Without belonging, what do you have? Chaos. Someone without proprioceptive qualities will, at times, lack awareness and control of the body. So, emotionally speaking, if you don't know where you are, where you fit in, or where you belong, there will, naturally, be chaos.

I don't want Kelly to feel like she wants to give up, and yet, I have felt exactly the same way with my own daughter. Exhaustion is normal. We adoptive parents may feel that way for several reasons: First, we are tired and don't see that we are making any progress. Second, at times we feel our efforts are futile. Third, we don't want to accept that parenting an adopted child is "different" than parenting a biological child. I believe the missing piece in the parent-child relationship is empathy. I can take a step back from my personal feelings, especially when my daughter is pushing my buttons, because I know where her anger, oppositional behavior, and fear are coming from.

It's not really a matter of her not wanting to fit in or get along. Instead, she's missing the internal emotional component that says: "This feels right, this is where you belong," and I completely get it. I would never expect someone who is permanently paralyzed to walk. I wouldn't get angry with him for not performing like someone who is not paralyzed. In the same way, it's more difficult for me to get angry with my daughter when I know she (at least right now) is not capable of the reciprocal love and acceptance that I would like for her to experience. I love and accept her anyway, exactly where she is, in hopes that she will someday have confidence that she belongs.

I do my best to hurt for her rather than be angry with her. Of course, we have some incredibly frustrating times, and that's when it's good to talk with a fellow adoptive parent who knows exactly what I'm feeling, who can empathize with me, and who won't judge me.

Escape to Whidbey Island

I escaped to Whidbey Island, Washington, for almost four weeks to pull some of my thoughts together about adoption, in general, and my specific experiences. Several people asked what I was doing while visiting for so long on the island. I told them, "Writing." If they asked what I was writing about, I explained.

I met an interesting couple while waiting to catch a bus. When they heard I was writing about adoption, they told me that they had spent some time in Cambodia teaching English, and that they had worked closely with an orphanage there. Seeing so many orphaned children pulled on their heartstrings, and they decided that when they were ready to have children, they would adopt. My comment to them was that while adoption is wonderful, it is also a roller coaster ride.

The husband said it might be difficult in unexpected ways for them since they had never been parents before. Even being prepared and expecting the ups and downs is still no comfort when the children actually come. It's really no comfort for the adopted child either. Somewhere in the back of my mind, I had this notion that because I was adopted, Maya would have an easier adjustment and more positive feelings about her adoption. My knowledge and understanding of what it felt like would somehow magically make her feelings disappear. This was wishful thinking, I suppose. I hoped that my understanding of her hurt and anger would ease her pain. It does not. It can't. She has to fight the battle to heal her own wounds. I'm here, willing to help however I can, but she must first be willing to go into battle and fight her own demons.

Without my own wounds, I suspect I might be less understanding, patient, and gentle with her as she tries to navigate life without her family of origin. I mentioned earlier that she had a meltdown while trying to write a letter to friends who were going to adopt. She has such a deep understanding about adoption issues and did an amazing job in the letter, articulately communicating her feelings. She wrote:

Dear Kevin and Annette,

When I heard that you were going to adopt, I had mixed emotions. It wasn't until I got home that I realized my emotions were coming from my own adoption. Most of the emotions I have, I don't understand. I, nor your adopted child, will fully comprehend what happened. Some days when I think about adoption, I am angry with myself for not being good enough for my birth parents to keep. On other days, I know that being adopted is a blessing.

Adoption is a big issue and also very complicated. Adopting is great because you are giving a child the love and guidance that they never got the chance to have. Adopting a child makes her feel more special than anybody. Adopting may solve your problem, but for the child, adoption doesn't change that much.

Even though I know that you will be amazing parents, your child will always have a safe and special place in her heart for her birth parents, and she will always have a hole in her that no adoptive parent can fill. As an adopted person, I question myself about who my parents were or maybe who I look like the most. I wonder a lot. When I was younger my parents took me to various people I could talk with about my adoption. The truth is that no one understands adoption unless they're adopted.

I'm adopted, and I still don't understand about adoption. At special times of the year, such as family times, I get temperamental, or most of the time I get sad. I don't understand these feelings that I have. The best thing for me was that my mom was always open, and she listened to everything I had to say. She was always there to help me.

Although even though I don't understand all of my adoption story, I know more of my adoption story than I think, and I am afraid of letting it out. I try as best as I can to push relationships away, because I don't want to be left alone again. If that happens and when it happens, you just gotta be there for your child and tell them that you love them.

Although I am fifteen, I still get that tiny thought in my mind that tells me that my adopted parents won't want me or that they might leave me somewhere and never come back. I do know that it has taken me a long time to open up to people, but I have recently opened up to my mom about my adoption fears. But I feel like if I have a real relationship with my mom, that I will lose her in some way, or something else. Anyway, I wrote this letter to help you recognize the roller coaster adoption really is, and that adoption defiantly [sic] won't be a piece of cake.
Sincerely,
Maya Decker

As I read Maya's letter, she kept asking me if it was okay. Twice she asked, "What's that look on your face?" I told her I was just soaking it all in, that it was a wonderful letter, and that I was amazed at how well she understood her emotions surrounding adoption. These are feelings I never could have articulated at the age of fifteen. She wrote: "and that adoption defiantly won't be a piece of cake." Now that's an interesting typo! "Defiantly." That's exactly how she approaches her adoption and the feelings that come with it.

I realize there is so much going on for her inside, on a daily basis, and how much she needs to be reassured that we will always be here. We are not going anywhere. She makes a poignant and bold statement when she says, "Adopting may solve your problem, but for the child, adoption doesn't change that much." I have some similar sentiments that may seem just as bold and possibly offensive, but let me back up a little.

When I think back to my grade school pictures, without even looking at them, I feel the weight of their sadness. It's as if the sadness has been stored in the photographs all these years, just waiting to be acknowledged. What I see in the eyes of the one staring back at me is a look of deep heartache and longing. I don't know how many of my grade school teachers made the comment, "Terri never smiles," and, "Terri needs to smile more." Smiling felt like a betrayal to me. To experience joy, happiness, pleasure—all a betrayal of the two-year-old who lost everything. Even though my brother and I were sent away together, it seems that we lost each other in all the confusion and chaos that surrounded us.

Carl, for some reason, appeared to be oblivious to what was going on. Why else would he, as my mother recounted, "...crawl up into a stranger's lap and say, I'm going home with you?'" I must have felt that I had no one to protect me, to stand with me in defiance of what was happening. So, it feels like all was lost, even though Carl was right there with me. It makes complete sense to me that I wasn't smiling in my grade school photographs, but no one bothered to find out or ask the question, "What's going on inside Terri? *Why* aren't you smiling?"

Without being drawn out, the feelings churned inside were being told to evaporate. Of course, feelings don't evaporate; they get buried. I believe that I lived through years of silenced pain and longing for my birth family. It took years before I actually smiled in one of my school pictures. This is not to say that I never, ever, smiled, but it does speak volumes that several of my teachers made comments about my melancholy disposition.

Even now, at times, my husband will say: "Smile." I don't; I usually glare back at him. That demand produces an allergic reaction within me. I want to erupt like a volcano of resentment. Smile? How could I? To do so would betray that little two-year-old. How could I smile, go on enjoying life, and have fun while she remains devastated? To happily accept this new life is to betray her. To trust another is betrayal. To put my heart and soul out there? To deeply love again? Betrayal.

The pictures look to me like I was someone who wanted to be freed. Be forewarned; this is the offensive part. Just keep in mind that I speak to myself as well because I am also an adoptive parent. When I look into that little girl's eyes in the school yearbook photos, all I see is a plea for help, for someone to listen ... to hear ... to take her back home where she belongs.

I'll never really feel like I belong where I am right now. It's like putting a wild animal in the zoo. All attempts are made at recreating the natural habitat, but the animal knows it's captive. How wonderful it is for us to see animals at the zoo that we would never otherwise encounter, but at the same time, how awful it is for animals to be taken out of their natural habitat, caged, and placed in a manipulated environment to make them feel like they're in the jungle. I am not saying that adopted children are placed into captivity. Obviously, they are in need of a home; I was in need of a home, and so was my daughter. What I am saying is that to the child, this home may not always feel like home. It isn't the child's natural habitat.

I appeal to adoptive parents to step out of their own experiences and try to empathize with their adopted children, not just at the beginning, but forever —because adoption is a lifelong journey.

Imagine if someone came into your home and took away your spouse or child. Then, he replaced the family member with someone of his own choosing and expected your life to go on without missing a beat.

Adopting may meet the want or need of the parent to have another child in the home. Adopting Maya met my desire to give a child a home, just like someone had done for me. Adopting her met my need to parent another child. Adopting Maya did not, as she wrote, meet all of her needs.

Her deepest need, as far as a family, is to be connected with her family of origin. It pulls at my heart to know that this is, in her case, just not possible.

Risky Relationships

Risk is a part of any meaningful relationship. If there is no risk whatsoever, there is little reason to attend to the relationship in the first place. Who you are and how you relate bears no consequence if there is no risk. It would be easy to take the relationship for granted; there is nothing to protect. In a parent-child relationship, fear of losing the relationship should not exist, but this is the foundational truth that I learned at a very early age. My family can abandon me. They did abandon me, and it could happen again. Not just that relationship, but any relationship holds the potential of cutting me off, leaving me alone.

I cannot grasp the idea of falling into a relationship and feeling complete oneness, harmony, and safety because the risk of losing that relationship is always lurking. One of the riskiest relationships I have is the one with Maya. There is often a tug of war between us. I am probably the riskiest relationship for her as well. One would think that Maya and I would bond deeply over shared insecurities as adoptees, but we don't always have that experience. I was vaguely aware of this risk when, one evening, Mark was reading a book by the fireplace in one of our over-stuffed rockers; I was in the other one. I decided to flip through the TV channels to see if I could catch a movie.

Enchanted was on with about an hour left. Maya and I had seen this together in the theater, so I called her down to see if she wanted to watch the rest of it with me. She came downstairs with an eager smile and plopped down next to me on the arm of the chair.

I wish I had this moment back; I would do it differently. If I had let her stay, she probably would have slid down next to me and shared the chair, resting partly on my lap. Instead, I told her not to sit on the arm of the chair, and to sit on the couch. I felt a twinge of guilt. I have sat on the arm of the chair before, so why did I send her to the couch? I briefly thought about asking her to join me in the chair, but didn't.

I know now that telling her to move wasn't at all about sitting on the arm of the chair. It was about not wanting to be too close to her. Not wanting the connection. I've never felt this danger with my other children, but with Maya it's different. Connecting with her is dangerous. Maybe because at any given moment she can (and often does) decide that she hates me, doesn't want to be around me, and that connecting with me is too dangerous for her. Allowing her to connect is more than dangerous, but I'm not sure what.

I have wondered why I feel this with her, and sometimes Mark, but not my boys. The subject came up with my therapist, and he suggested that marriage is much like an adoption. It is welcoming someone, unrelated, into your life—making them "family." So, not only is Maya an adopted relative, so is Mark.

I had never thought of it this way before, but it makes complete sense. It does not, however, feel like a relationship that I can "fall into," as mentioned earlier. It is one that needs caution, protection, and a defensive stand. The desire for intimacy and connection is surely there, just like in a biological family, but because this connection has been broken once, I feel I must be on my guard to not let it happen again. One of the fears that has been with me as long as I can remember is getting close to someone, intimately connecting, and fitting together like a pretty mosaic, and then something dreadful happens. Life is shattered. The person is taken from life or takes his or her life and leaves to create another mosaic ... with someone else.

The more intimate the connection, the greater the risk is. An even greater fear is that those close to me will be involved in an accident or become deathly ill once intimacy is cultivated and thriving. I'd rather have distant and here than intimate and gone.

I remember thinking at a very early age, "people I care about get taken away." So, being distant, in general, is safer. Maya too, I believe, participates in this dance between closeness and distance.

Maya was tasked with painting a family circle for art class. When I learned she was working on this activity, I was excited to see it. I was confident that I would be the family member closest to her. Maya is in the center, a turquoise dot. According to my prediction, I would be the yellow dot—which looks like a peanut shell. To my surprise, there are two dots there; one is Lia, and one is Sheila (Maya's two friends from the orphanage in India). It's interesting that she put them so close together because whenever we get together, Lia and Sheila seem to be more closely connected, with Maya on the periphery.

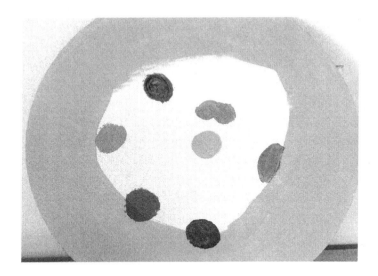

I was a bit surprised that they even made it into our family circle, especially when I have to nudge Maya to e-mail or send them messages on Facebook. It's a toss-up as to who is more connected to Maya.

The only one not touching the outside turquoise line is the navy-blue dot at the top. This may be Matt, our oldest son, but I don't remember. I could go through every dot, but I'll cut to the chase—I'm the purple one at the bottom, the one farthest away and also the one that is less than halfway in the white area. I have mixed feelings about this, and I suppose I shouldn't be surprised about my "placement," but I am.

I understand Maya more than anyone in our family. I pray she knows and feels this. I don't want her to feel distant from me. At times, the effort in wrapping my arms around her, to help her feel connected to me and the family who loves her seems futile. Will she ever feel safely connected to me? Will I to her?

We were shopping at a thrift shop one week for some clothes, and Maya was having a great time (and she doesn't like to shop). Her exact words were, "This is fun." Something in me was cautious, pulling back just a bit, with an inner voice saying, "Don't have too much fun with her, you know what happens whenever we have a good time." How crazy is that? Who thinks that way about their children? Don't have too much fun, get too close, don't have a deep bond and attachment. I want all those things, yet when Maya verbalized enjoyment in what we were doing together, the internal alarms went off. Often what happens after we've had an enjoyable time together is sabotage on her part. It's exactly what she wrote about in her letter to the adoptive couple at church. "If I get too close, I will lose the relationship."

Relationships are a quandary. It feels dangerous to have fun, be comforted, to entertain the thought of needing or allowing myself to relax in another person's arms and have that need met. Even more dangerous is someone else knowing that I have this need for connection and that they might actually be giving me what I need. Hiding my needs has become second nature. To make my needs known and then not have them met would be unbearable. I "needed" to be returned to my home when I was two, and no one was listening. It became safer to not have any needs.

Thoughts on Attachment

I probably formed some kind of attachment as an infant, but I'm just not sure to whom. Most likely, I would guess, I attached to my grandmother. My mother says that we were close. I've read how some adoptees, when reuniting with their birthmothers, want to touch, be close, have their mothers hold them. I have never felt this way. Could it be because I was never attached to her in the first place? Was she distant?

The scenario I imagine is that she was desperate to get away from home. One child didn't get her far enough away, so she began chasing after her "boyfriend" (who wasn't hanging around much anymore), and got pregnant again with me. Having two children together would surely lure him into a permanent relationship. Her plan backfired, and he was never to be seen again. Now, she was stuck with my brother *and* me. She really did not want to be pregnant. She wanted a man to take her away from the misery of her family life. Once I was born, and my father had yet to show his face, the reality of being a single, teenage mom of two children began to sink in.

I wonder what it was like for her to look me in the eye each day. Maybe she didn't. If she was saddled before, now there was a ball and chain around her neck. She must have despised me for it. It makes sense that I would not be attached to her. She must have gladly given parental responsibilities over to anyone who would offer assistance—even her mother, with whom she had a volatile relationship.

Could it be that her ambivalence bred mine? I wonder if attachment works that way. Of course, I don't really know if she was ambivalent toward me. This is merely conjecture on my part. For two years she played the role of mother, I'm just not sure in what capacity. I wonder when she began thinking about giving us up. Was it her idea? Someone in the family? Possibly, it was more of an ultimatum, as in, "If you're not going to be the mother, then...." This early broken attachment has had lasting effects.

Connections

When reflecting on one's family, I'm assuming that you could point to one or several people in that family with whom you have a deep connection. As I personally reflect in that way, I can't say that I was close to any of my siblings—not even my biological brother, nor did I have a deep connection to either of my parents.

When I began to think about the school friends that I connected with, I had an epiphany. I was drawn to the "bad" kids, those kids who liked to "live on the edge." One of my grade school friends was Mavis Maye. Mavis was the daughter of a Nazarene preacher. She liked to live big, and she didn't have to fly under the radar like I did. She was fun to be with and always looking for an adventure. In the third grade, we would each leave the room for a different reason. One of us would ask to go get a drink, and the other would ask to go use the restroom. We would meet at the restroom with our glow-in-the-dark super-balls, charge them, turn off the lights, and then throw them against the brick walls and watch the flying light show. We ceased this particular adventure when on one occasion, Mavis flushed the toilet with her foot, and it slipped into the toilet.

Another adventure took place at lunch recess in the sixth grade. Our school sat on a large piece of property bordering a railroad track. A swath of trees and brush separated the school grounds from the train tracks. It was easily accessible, with foot paths here and there that kids used to take short-cuts home. We were supposed to be on school grounds, not in the wooded area, but that's where we were. Mavis, another friend, I'll call her Lizzy, and I were outside the boundaries. I was wearing my bright red-orange, shiny, patent leather coat. I spread the coat, using it as a wind block so Mavis could light some cigarettes. So much for camouflage! Of course I didn't smoke any of the cigarettes, nor did I want to; I hated the smell of smoke. I was drawn to the daring escapade. We were spotted (who could miss that bright red coat?) by a parent volunteer. I escaped any consequences since I did no smoking. I remained safe by flying under the radar once again.

We were also big on daring one another to pull crazy stunts. I knew better than to accept a dare, but I did hand out a few. On one occasion I dared someone, maybe Lizzy, to pour a carton of milk down the tuba in the band room. The band room was also the stage, which was open to the gym, which at lunchtime served as the cafeteria. One could grab a carton of milk and slip in without anyone ever noticing. The dare was accepted. Not only did she pour the milk in, but she also stuffed the empty milk carton down the bell of the tuba. I gave no thought to what damage might be done, if any, to the tuba. If one of my own children were to pull such a stunt I would probably be asking incredulously, "What were you thinking?"

We escaped any consequences until the next dare was accepted and exposed. I made a monumental and life-saving decision to go home after school this particular day, and luckily, was not present for the dare of all dares. Mavis and Lizzy stayed behind, loitering around the school building. I'm not sure what prompted Mavis to do it, but she dared Lizzy to remove her clothes and run around the gym naked. More surprising is that Lizzy took her up on the dare. This was in 1973, a year before streaking became popular. She was on the cutting edge. As Lizzy began her streak around the gym, the principal just happened to be walking by outside and saw her through the glass doors. He began banging on the locked doors yelling, "You get your clothes on!"

I think teachers and administrators were happy to see our class graduate to junior high. By high school, Mavis had moved, and my best buddy was Darcy. She, too, liked to live wild. The most daring prank she pulled was accomplished without my help—not because I wouldn't have joined her, but because I simply didn't hear the doorbell ring when she came to my house looking for me. For some reason, she decided to egg our basketball coach's car. I remember neither of us were too fond of her, but I don't know that we had any good reason for our shared dislike. Darcy was sure that the coach was out of town for the weekend, so she drove over to her house, pulled up behind her parked car, and decorated it with a dozen eggs. Unfortunately for Darcy, the coach was in town and watching from her apartment window.

Darcy was promptly removed from the basketball team. At the time, I didn't know what the big deal was over such a harmless prank. I didn't know the damage eggs would do to a car's paint job. Had Darcy known, she probably wouldn't have followed through with her plan. I believe I wanted to live on-the-edge, but the closest I got was choosing friends who did live on the edge. I followed them but remained safe in their shadows, I was close enough to feel the thrill of the adventure, yet I never jumped in with both feet.

Knowing You vs. Knowing About You

I came across the following paragraph in a novel by Per Petterson that gave me pause. From *Out Stealing Horses*:

> *People like it when you tell them things, in suitable portions, in modest, intimate tone, and they think they know you, but they do not, they know about you, for what they are let in on are facts, not feelings, not what your opinion is about anything at all, not how what has happened to you and how all the decisions you have made have turned you into who you are. What they do is they fill in with their own feelings and opinions and assumptions, and they compose a new life which has precious little to do with yours, and that lets you off the hook. No-one can touch you unless you yourself want them to.*

I read it over several times thinking, *YES. That's me. That describes my interactions with people; this is how I have learned to be in relationships.* I don't know when it started, but it is something that must have grown, layer upon layer. Most people who know me well, and some not so well, know that I am adopted. They know most of the facts, like how old I was, that my brother was adopted with me, that there are three other adopted siblings in our family, and so on. But none of them know how this life event has turned my whole being upside down. It's a reflex just to give out factual information. I responded that way for so long that I identified only with the facts of the situation and not the feelings

I will probably never forget the day someone said to me, "I know and have talked to a lot of people who are adopted, and I know how they feel, but I don't know how you feel about being adopted." The remark caught me off guard. I wasn't sure how I really felt about it. I had never allowed myself to explore my feelings about adoption, at least not in any depth. I felt panic creep over me. I realized in that moment that I didn't know how I felt, and if I didn't figure it out, and quickly, that I couldn't be helped. This fear was a powerful motivator.

I sat down and began writing several pages about the feelings related to my adoption (I might even be able to add some things to the list now, two years later). As I write this now, we are in a gorgeous setting—a wide beach, comfortable condominium, warm weather, etc., and I realize that even here, with my own husband and children, I communicate in facts.

Mark brought this to my attention as we were walking along the beach. He had repeated for about the fourth time, "This is such a nice view." I asked him why he kept making the same comment, and he remarked, "Because I don't know how you feel about it. I don't know what you're thinking." Sometimes I don't really stop to consider a situation, and when I do, I often wonder if others would clearly understand my thoughts. Often, I feel like I will have to defend my thoughts and feelings, and I'm so unsure of them at times, I avoid sharing them. On another trip, I began to feel oddly out of place. This was a new sensation for me because with my husband and children, I have always belonged. As the boys have grown and become more independent, their relationships with each other have grown as well. They enjoy being with each other. They don't need mom and dad so much anymore to help them negotiate.

One day during the trip, the boys had been playing football on the beach, swimming in the ocean, playing cards, climbing palm trees to pick coconuts, and so on. I enjoyed watching them hang out together, but at the same time, I felt like an outsider. This is a recurring theme for me, and I wonder if it will ever resolve itself.

It takes enormous amounts of trust for me to tell someone about who I am beyond the facts. This is especially true when they do not share my experiences. I remember telling a friend that my early loss made trusting other people difficult. She said, "Not to minimize *your* loss, but everyone deals with loss." On one hand, she is exactly right. Everyone deals with loss at some point in life, but not everyone deals with it in the dramatic and frightening way I did.

These are the kinds of statements that keep me from sharing more than the facts. I don't want to have to defend myself. I have ignored them for so long that now, when they begin to surface, it is easy to question their validity. As I feel the emotions rise from the depths, I am filled with self- doubt. In the third book of *The Hunger Games*, Peeta is captured by the Capitol. While captive, he is tortured by having his memories distorted and twisted to the point that he no longer knows what is real. Friends become the enemy; those he once loved and cared for become his assassination targets. His friends have to reconstruct his memory for him and continually tell him if a situation, thought, or idea is real or not. He waivers between reality and falsehood. I understand Peeta's struggle with reality. Is it real, true, that I have little or no emotion connected to my past? Is it true that it really doesn't affect me, that I have accepted it, and that I have moved on? Or, has my birth family's relinquishment affected me deeply, and I am now just beginning to unearth, one by one, the slivers?

I believe it is the latter; the trauma greatly affected me, yet I still waiver at times, marching with the flag of "I'm fine, it doesn't bother me, —I'm unaffected." While life used to be safer when I functioned in quiet, life is now becoming more painful and exhausting when I hold up the "denial flag."

Chosen, Loved, yet Conflicted

I never imagined that having a family of my own would surface buried emotions connected with my adoption history. In writing about my three sons living twelve hours away, familiar adoption terms I use began to surface: *disheartening, disconnected, diminished, replaced, displaced, outside looking in.* No matter how many times I tell myself otherwise or try to convince myself that I am worth keeping, the nagging evidence looms in my mind. "But you were chosen," someone might argue. This argument is flawed. To be chosen by someone outside of your family of origin means that you were discarded, not wanted, by your own flesh and blood.

This primal wounding does not fade like a newly acquired tan. The effects are permanent—not that healing is impossible, but there is permanent scarring. I am reminded of a talk I had with my mother about this topic. She was relaying a conversation she had with our grade school principal sometime after my brother had started kindergarten.

School was a challenge for him, and he was struggling on many fronts. The principal, insightful and empathetic, said something to the effect of, "Remember, he's just lost his mother." The school of thought at the time was that children are resilient, so just give them a home and they'll be fine. This is the paradigm that many social workers and adoptive parents bought into.

My mother was simply going along with the working theory of the time when she responded to the principal by saying, "Oh, he has a mother now." She meant, "He's just fine. The past is just that, in the past, so losing his mother doesn't matter now." I suppose that may work with pets when they are taken from the litter, but that does not work with people. A surrogate mother is not the same as the original. I can say this with complete confidence because I am one. How I have often wished that just my presence and love for Maya were all that was needed and could wash away the hurt and pain of losing her first mother.

Recently, Maya and I were in a heated discussion about homework. She asked me to proofread a paper. I did, and she didn't care too much for the corrections I suggested. The conversation quickly went from homework to, "You always correct me and tell me everything I do wrong."

I apologized to her, telling her that I don't want her to feel like she gets only correction. I followed this by telling her how frustrating it is for me sometimes because whenever I (or her dad) try to compliment her, she argues with the compliment. The conversation quickly turned as she began to cry and say the whole thing was her fault. She explained that she really doesn't want to hear the compliments from her dad or me. She wants to hear them from her birthparents. Once again, I am stunned by her self-awareness. Mother's Day was just two days away, and perhaps that triggered her volatile emotions.

I talked to her about how much it stinks. The past and all its hurt are not erased simply because she has a family now. "I know it stinks. I'm sorry I can't make it all better. I wish I could."

"It's not fair that the boys get to know their birthmother and I don't. I don't want to meet her; I just want a picture of her," she replied.

I validated how unfair it is, how other kids don't have to feel what she feels, that they don't know the pain of being "unwanted" for whatever reason. Is there a good one? A justifiable one? I told her how sorry I was that I can't reflect to her who she is, like her birthmother would be able to do. She certainly doesn't get her pretty brown skin, silky black hair, and contagious smile, with its perfectly placed dimple, from me.

She lamented, "God doesn't love me. My shadow is too dark."

I reminded her that great light casts great shadows.

I received a slight smile. She came and sat in my lap. She was sixteen then. We were almost twelve years post-adoption, but the pain was still there. I held her in my lap and mused about my own Mother's Day misgivings.

Mother's Day is difficult for me, too, not because I don't like being a mother—it's absolutely wonderful—but because one mother gave me up and the other is supposed to do the impossible: make up for it.

There are absolutely no Mother's Day cards to be found that could even begin to express the confusion and conflicts I feel surrounding the day. Another flawed sentiment is, "She loved you so much, she gave you up." I've never been able to wrap my mind around that statement, even as an adult. How could anyone expect a child to accept it as a reasonable explanation for being relinquished. It reaches the apex of all oxymora. So, the things I love, I give away? Then there is no permanency in love, no grounding, no security. I believe this is the wrong message to send to any adopted child.

Swallowing

There are only a few events that I remember while growing up when I allowed myself an outward display of emotions. When I was around twelve, the movie *Brian's Song* was on television. As the true story of the young football player's battle with cancer unfolded, I was overcome with emotion, and not with a few tears. The loss felt personal. I couldn't stop the flood. I appeared to be the only one moved by the movie. I remember a few snickers from the family, and I felt foolish for allowing my emotions to take over.

Another time, we were at my aunt and uncle's house watching *The Ghost and Mr. Chicken*. For some reason, I was standing up near the back of the family room. Behind me was a hallway that led to bedrooms and a bath. During a suspenseful part in the movie, just as the music began to get louder and the anticipation heightened, my uncle grabbed me from behind, eliciting a scream and tears. Everyone laughed. I didn't think it was funny.

Even now, I do not like to be jumped at in the dark. The last time Mark tried to spook me, I came out swinging. He doesn't do it anymore. I will, from time to time, be teased about these two events when the entire family is together. The message I received growing up was that it was not okay to show emotion. Being sad, angry, or afraid is weak. We'd better just swallow all that nonsense.

Excavating memories and unhealed sentiments over the last several years has been difficult. Denying that any troublesome emotions exist and forcing them back down if they begin to surface has been my modus operandi. Angry? No, of course not. Sad? No, I'm perfectly fine. Afraid (of being rejected)? No way! Why would I be afraid of that? Push it all back down. Deny, deny, deny.

Oddly enough, I recently developed some strong food allergies. I was beginning to feel like something was stuck in my throat whenever I ate. I drank glass after glass of water, but it would not go down. I had a barium swallow test done and everything looked good, yet I continued to have this "stuck" feeling, and it was getting worse. A chiropractor suggested I get an endoscopy. I did, and the doctor found scarring from my esophagus to my small intestine. He suggested allergies of some kind. I had blood tests done to determine what I was allergic to and ended up with a list of thirty-three food allergens. Yeast and gluten were two of the biggest culprits. I had the most trouble after eating bagels, bread, muffins, and similar foods. Once I eliminated these from my diet, I happily felt the symptoms disappear.

I wonder if these sudden food allergies are somehow related to my recent exploration of feelings so long denied. I contemplate the idea of being angry, only to deny and push the feelings back down. Feelings, like food, seem to be stuck inside. Getting beneath the mantra of "everything is fine" is another layer that needs to be peeled away.

The Search for My Father

I didn't think of my biological father too often while I was growing up (maybe not at all). What is unique about the connection to our mothers? About five years after I met my birthmother, I became curious about my birthfather. His name was on my original birth certificate (the real one, not the one that says I was born to my adoptive parents).

Once I had it in hand, I could begin searching for him. I had never laid eyes on my original birth certificate and didn't even know it existed until after I told my adoptive parents that I had searched for and found my birthmother.

I was thirty-one years old before I saw my original birth certificate. Imagine! I studied it over and over again. There are still times when I go to the fire safe to take it out and study it, each time thinking that I might have missed some nugget of information. It is one of the only pieces of my life that feels authentic. That might sound strange, but not to someone who has struggled with questions like, "Who am I," and, "Where do I belong," all her life.

Some time passed after we adopted Maya, and then I began searching for my father. I did a Google search, but it produced nothing. I tried a search engine that finds basic information about people and thought I had found the right person. There was an e-mail associated with his name, so I sent him an e-mail. I set up an entirely separate e-mail account—I wasn't sure I wanted him to know my last name and my existing account would have given this away. I checked the account daily for several weeks. Then I checked once a week, then checked every other week, and eventually, I let several months go by without checking to see if he had responded. After a long time, I decided to check the account again, but to my chagrin, I had forgotten the password and hadn't written it down anywhere. I worked for days trying several possibilities, but never was able to recall what it was. To my knowledge, he has never responded. I was never able to confirm that this e-mail really belonged to my birthfather in the first place.

About five years later, I tried again. I was in the kitchen, sitting at the computer desk. Mark was out of town, and the kids were home from school and enjoying a snack at the table. I casually typed his name in again, expecting to get nothing, but this time, his obituary popped up. I was stunned. It took my breath away. I remember thinking, *No, this can't be. It's not supposed to happen this way.* I sat in silence, staring at the computer screen with the realization sinking in that I will never meet my birthfather, ever. And he will never meet me. I read and re-read the obituary several times, soaking it all in. I learned about his survivors—his wife, daughter, grandchildren, sister, and brothers. I decided to initiate contact with one of his brothers to see if he would send me a few pictures. It was easy to find his phone number but not easy to place the call. I had no idea if my birthfather's brothers and sister even knew about me. I was born in Michigan, and they lived in West Virginia. I called anyway.

The phone rang, and someone answered—no turning back now. I eased into the subject of who I was and why I was calling. I was speaking with Frank, my father's stepbrother. He said he remembered my brother and me. He gave me the following sketchy details about my birthfather: My birthfather and his mother were abandoned by my birth grandfather when my birthfather was young. My birth grandmother remarried, and her new husband (Frank's father) raised my birthfather as his own. It struck me how my own father had been abandoned, and then, probably for reasons I will never know, became the abandon-er. Frank briefly told me about my birthfather's illness that led to his death. By the end of the conversation, I was hopeful, expecting to receive at least a few pictures of this mystery man.

Several weeks, then months passed, and nothing came. I sent Frank a note with my address, thanking him in advance for being helpful and sending pictures. Again, nothing. I considered contacting my birthfather's daughter (my sister) but decided against it. I didn't want to invade her life. The chances were good that she knew nothing about me. I let it go for several years, and then the idea of contacting her began gnawing at me. The thought kept going through my mind, *If I had a sister out there, I would want to know, regardless of the circumstances.* I realize this comes from my struggle with belonging. I doubt this is a struggle she shares, and she may have no desire to know anything about me.

Moses

I was reading in Exodus one day and came across the story of Moses. Exodus 2:11-12 (NLT) reads, "One day, after Moses had grown up, he went out to where his own people were and watched them at their hard labor. He saw an Egyptian beating a Hebrew, one of his own people. Looking this way and that and seeing no one, he killed the Egyptian and hid him in the sand."

I wonder what prompted Moses to go out that particular day and watch his people. I can imagine a few of the thoughts that went through his mind as he watched them. Maybe he thought, *That's where I should be. Those are my people, and that's where I really belong. I'm glad I'm not a slave. I feel guilty for not being enslaved along with my own family. I wonder if they hate me for not being mistreated along with them. I miss them. I wish I could be with my family but not give up the family I have now. Why me? I wonder if my family misses me. Do they wish to be with me? Have they tried to contact me? My life is so easy and theirs so difficult. They don't deserve to be mistreated, beaten. You (Egyptians) have taken something away from me. You are going to pay for it (with your lives).*

No one can begin to know all that Moses felt and pondered as he grew up in Pharaoh's household. And look at the trouble HIS unbridled emotions got him into—murder, a cover-up, and fleeing for his life! Clearly (to me) he had no one to talk to about all of his feelings. Why else would he go out and watch his own people? He must have led a very lonely life, and then when he fled to Midian in fear of Pharaoh, he became a shepherd watching over the flocks of his father-in-law, which brought about more solitude. The naming of his first son, Gershom speaks volumes about his loneliness. *Gershom* means *I have become a foreigner in a foreign land.* The truth is, Moses was a foreigner in his own land before he became a foreigner in a foreign land. The loneliness stacked up for him.

Reading about Moses prompted me to go out and watch (search for) my people, so to speak. Watching today though is more high-tech than in Moses' time. I began searching on Facebook for my sister because we have the same birth father. I was pretty sure I found her and then started weighing whether or not I should send her a message. I had her home address and phone number for some time. I tried to call her once and I eventually sent her a message on Facebook but never got any answer, so I dropped it.

Being reminded of Moses, something pushed me over the edge, and I sent her another message. I felt mischievousness about the whole thing. I wasn't looking to give her a heart attack or anything, but what I wouldn't have given to be a fly on the wall when she opened up that message! I just had to wait and see what would happen, it could be wonderful or disastrous. Something told me I could handle disastrous.

I sent her the following message:

Dear Rona, I have known of you for several years and finally decided to try and contact you. I was doing a web search for my biological father when, regrettably, his obituary popped up. As I read it, I learned that he had another daughter (you). (If Connor is not your father, then I have the wrong Rona). Maybe you have known that he had two children (I have an older brother) before he had a family with your mother, or this may be a complete shock. I would love to talk to you more. I'm especially hoping to see a picture of my biological father someday, too. I talked to Frank on the phone a few years ago about sending me a picture, but he never sent one. If you choose, you can respond via Facebook or my e-mail: _____ I hope to hear from you.

I waited almost a year but heard nothing. In December 2011, I decided to send an e-mail to Rona, using her work e-mail address. This time, much to my surprise, I heard back from her.

Dear Terri, I did receive your email on Facebook at the beginning of the year and chose to ignore it. It was nothing against you and your brother. It was out of respect for my mother. My uncle Frank did not mention anything to me about your request. He talks to my mother quite often and she did not mention anything to me about it either. My mother knows about your brother, but I don't know if she knows about you; I am not even sure if my father knew about you. I am sorry that it took you so long to find your birth parents. That must have been a very long and difficult process, needless to say, very emotional. Frank may have told

131

you a little bit about our family. I am an only child, been married for twenty-seven years to a wonderful man with whom I have known since we were fifteen. He is from (_____) but we met in (_____) at the YMCA. We have two beautiful children. They both are very ambitious, industrious young people and we are very proud of them. They were my father's life. Daddy was an intelligent man even though he did not complete school.

He left West Virginia when he was very young. He and my mother met in Chicago and were married there. My mother is from Ohio but was in Illinois for job opportunities. She worshiped the ground my father walked on and is still not over his death. He was diagnosed with diabetes in the mid-seventies and was not managed well by his physician. In the late 1990s, his kidney function, visual acuity and other major organs were affected by his diabetes. He went on dialysis in 2003 and really surprised me that he decided to, but he wanted to see our children graduate from high school) and then passed away in 2006.

He was a wonderful husband and father. He always provided us with the things we needed. He was a workaholic until he became so ill that he couldn't work. He was very humorous and witty. He was a very faithful man to Jesus in his later years.

I had looked at your pictures on Facebook when you emailed me earlier in the year. You have features that remind me of Daddy's mother, aunt, and sisters. I will try to find some pictures of Daddy for you.

I am not very savvy with Facebook yet, but my best friend has taken some of her old family photographs and posted them. Maybe she can help me do this for you. I would love to hear about your family. I know you have children. I apologize again for not getting back with you. I still need to talk to Mom about the contact you have made with me. I hope you have a wonderful holiday.

I had several feelings swirling around after reading her e-mail. I was touched by the richness of her response, so full of details about her life and her family. I realize she did not have to share any of that with me. I was also hurt by her initial decision to ignore my previous e-mail. I completely understood her desire to respect and be sensitive to her mother, but at the same time, I felt dismissed. I was pleased that she chose to respond this time but also cautious not to push or expect something from her that she was not ready or willing to give. I sent Rona an e-mail telling her briefly about my own family and expressing my desire for her to do what was best for her mother. Her next e-mail, again, was full of information about her life and an abundance of identifying information. She said that finding out about me, "stirred emotions in [her] inner being that [she] couldn't express."

Some of the stories didn't add up. My uncle (Frank) said he remembered both my brother and me. My sister said she wasn't sure that my father even knew about me. Rona and I are close in age; I am only nine months older than she is. Same father, different mothers—a sticky situation to say the least. Rona's doubts about my birthfather's knowledge of me stirred emotions for me as well. How could he have a child and not know about it? I know it happens all the time, but when it happens to you, it seems impossible. This also speaks to my sense of worth. I'm not worth knowing or being acknowledged by my own father. As I read about how involved he was as a grandfather, irritation and anger rose within me. "They were his life," she wrote about his grandchildren. Well, he has three more biological grandsons who have missed out on his love and devotion.

Half-Sister

I have two sisters in my adoptive family. Neither of them is biologically related to me. I wondered for many years if it were possible that I had a sister somewhere out there. Correction: I have *three* sisters. So here's what's bugging me. Others have referred to my brother (whom I met seventeen years ago) as my "half-brother." We have the same mother but different fathers. And now that I have made contact with my sister (same father, different mother ... this could get really complicated) a few have referred to her as my half-sister.

How is it, I wonder, that the two sisters who have absolutely no shared biological ties are my sisters, and the one who is actually *biologically related* to me is only my "half-sister." I know such comments are innocent, but hearing them irritates me.

The concept is that I'm being forced into a relationship with my siblings from my adoption while my biological siblings don't really count. They are not recognized as true, full, siblings. It's probably trivial on my part, but whenever I hear references to half-siblings, a little fireball starts churning inside.

In a strange way, I'm being told that I'm not a whole person. I remember a friend saying something about my half-brother one time, and I said, "You know, he's more my brother than my adopted siblings are."

It went right over her head. She continued to refer to him as "half" whenever the subject came up. It probably shouldn't bother me, but it does.

Silent Fathers

The timeline that I have pieced together points to the growing possibility that my father did not even know I existed. I still have doubts about this, which may come from a deep yearning and longing for him to know and to care. The silence of my biological father troubles me and gnaws at my sense of worth and value. It seems to me that his life was fragmented. The description given to me by Rona is that he was a great provider and family man. I have trouble integrating this perception of my biological father. He was never there for me, and the son that he did know about, he abandoned. Which person is he? Great family man or abandoner?

My adoptive father is the silent type. He has many admirable qualities. He is calm, easy-going, and organized to a fault. I used to think it was so funny that he would separate his potato chips according to size before eating them. He was never at a loss to find what he needed, so his organization skills served him well. Dad was disciplined and a hard worker. I don't ever remember him calling in to work because he was sick. He kept his feelings and emotions to himself. I never saw him get angry, but I also never saw him cry. Not even when his father died. I remember him being very matter of fact about it, which puzzled me. I came home from an all-night New Year's Eve party to hear my mom talking on the phone about grandpa, "... heart attack ... falling down the steps...."

I said to my dad: "Grandpa had a heart attack? Is he okay?" My dad said, "No, he's dead." I don't know what affected me more—the death of my grandfather or my dad's lack of emotion about it. Probably the latter. I certainly remember that brief exchange more vividly than I remember my grandfather's funeral.

I enjoyed playing catch with dad in the back yard, along with tossing the football, and shooting games of basketball. We often played ping-pong, and I was never able to beat him. He seemed to play so effortlessly, while I was desperately trying to get just one win. Actually, I'm glad I never beat him. I'm not sure why that matters, but it does. His silence is different than that of my biological father. He is present but also distant. I don't really know him. I don't know what makes him joyful, angry, or sad. I don't know what moves his soul. I don't know what he thinks of me, my life, or my family.

How sad it is to be raised by someone yet not know him. It takes something from your soul. I have no memories of walking with him, holding his hand, or of being carried in his arms. These gestures were too expressive for him. I wish I had more to write about him, but what do you say about a man about whom you know very little? In some ways, he is a stranger, much like the father I never met.

More From My Sister

Rona and I became Facebook friends, but otherwise our communication went silent for over five years. In the back of my mind, I always felt that when her mother passed, she would likely get in touch with me.

I think about all the things we do for those we love. We keep silent about concerns, feelings, hurts, disappointments—all to "protect." I kept my search for my birthmother a secret from my adoptive parents to protect them. Was I protecting them or me? I told myself it was to protect them, but in hindsight I think I felt responsible for their feelings, or what I thought their feelings might be. I've learned, and sometimes have to remind myself, that others are responsible for their own feelings; I am responsible only for mine.

The years passed, and I waited.

August 14, 2016, Rona posted a picture of her dad on Facebook around Father's Day. I sent another message, "Hi Rona, just saw your "dad" post on Facebook and didn't want to comment publicly, but I would still love to have a picture of my own father if you are willing to share. My home address is …."

There was no response, so I waited.

It was late afternoon on May 1, 2020, when my messenger tone sounded. It was Rona! She wrote, "I imagine you wonder why I am contacting you now. I did an Ancestry DNA, and it looks like you are my closest relative that has done this testing. I have a question. You mentioned a brother in one of the first emails that you sent to me. Where is he, or do you have contact with him?"

I replied, "We were adopted into the same family. He is two years older than I am. He lives in Bloomington, Illinois, just an hour from me. We don't have much contact—long story. His name is Carl."

Rona wrote back, "I'm sorry that I didn't delve more into our relationship before. As I told you, my mom was suffering from such great depression over Daddy's death. I just couldn't put her through it. She passed away last June. She had a scheduled hip replacement and then had MRSA septicemia. While all that was going on, our son Robert was diagnosed with a brain tumor. Benign, thank God! It has been quite the year. He lives in Florida with our only grandchild who is now eighteen months old."

I wrote, "I knew that your mother was a great concern, and I figured that had a lot to do with your silence. I completely understand. I saw the posts about Robert too. So glad the news was a relief to your family. Grandchildren are the best! We have three grandsons in Woodstock, Georgia, (from our oldest son Matthew) and one on the way from our middle son, Andrew, who lives in Smyrna, Georgia.

Rona wrote back, "It seems we have two other siblings. I received another email at work about five years ago. The man that contacted me then asked questions about Daddy being friends with two men whose names I can't remember, [asked if he was] from Bradshaw, West Virginia, and if he had lived in Chicago. So I asked mom about it. She didn't know about him but then told me about you and your brother and that you both would visit at Daddy's mother's house."

This last text took my breath away. I used to visit my grandparents' home? Was my father there? How long did we stay? How did we get there? We lived in Trenton, Michigan. Bradshaw, West Virginia, would have been over a seven-hour drive. So many questions, so few answers.

I wrote back to her, "Your mom knew about us?" Rona answered, "When Daddy met Mom in May of 1960, and they were about to get married, Daddy said he could possibly have a son. Mom told him that they could raise him as their own if he wanted. He said he wasn't sure if the boy was his or not. I just assumed that was your brother."

"What a sweet mom you were blessed with."

"Yes ... it upset me at the time because they hadn't told me about you all ... they had told me about the boy ... said his name was Doug. So, this boy that Daddy told Mom about did exist. I had a young lady text me from Florida that told me she thought I was her dad's half-sister ... she also knew names, places, etc. She now works in the same town where Robert lives ... what are the chances of that?!?!?! Then to add icing on the cake, he passed away in November. Doug also lived near our son. He was born in 1957.

I asked, "So, who is the other sibling?"

She wrote, "The one that emailed me ... his name is Reid ... he lives in Indiana ... I've been in contact with him. He was adopted as well ... so it seems that there was Doug - March 1957, Carl - July 1959, Reid - December 1960, you - January 1961, and then me - October 1961 ... if all the genetics prove.

Fascinated, I wrote, "Wow! How did you find Reid?"

She said, "This has been so much to digest. Reid says his mother was growing in her faith when he turned fifty, and she told him all about it. He said he

141

thought something wasn't right growing up, but never mentioned it out of respect for her ... so then he contacted me through my work email, just like you—"

"His adoptive mom? You mean he didn't know he was adopted?"

"He was raised by his biological mother, not father. I'm sorry to be throwing all of this at you at once—"

I said, "No worries. It's actually wonderful to hear from you, but so sorry you are dealing with so much all at once."

She said, "It's okay. I figured it would all come together at some point. I was messaging Reid last night. He ordered a DNA kit ... I encouraged the young lady to do so as well ... So, I guess me being an only child is not a true statement anymore."

More of the Story

I was always curious about what had prompted my mother to send us to an orphanage, abandon us, give us up, relinquish her rights (there are so many ways to say it). It took several decades for me to begin wondering the same thing about my birthfather. What was it about his life and experiences that made it okay for him to have very little or nothing to do with us? Now this question includes Doug and Reid, as well as Carl and me.

Rona's brief history of my birthfather shed a little light on my question. She shared the following:

> *This is part of his story. His mother, Mira Mumford, was fifteen when Daddy was born. My father's biological father was twenty-one. They didn't marry. Daddy never spoke to him—probably because 'Mommaw' wouldn't let him. She was a piece of work. That's another long story. Anyway, she met and married a wonderful man named John P. He wanted to adopt Daddy but couldn't afford to, but he raised Daddy as his own. He treated me as if I were his biological granddaughter. I never knew the difference until I was about thirteen. I thought Daddy's name was different because she was married before.*

It makes a little more sense to me now. A man abandoned by his own father as a young boy simply repeated his own history. This is what he knew as a child. He also did not get along well with his mother (according to Rona), and he left home at the young age of sixteen. There are so many questions and mysteries

143

surrounding his history and Edith's, many of which may never be answered.

As Rona and I continued our chat via Messenger, I mentioned that we were planning an impromptu trip to the North Georgia mountains. We had rented a secluded cabin because we needed to escape our Covid-19 seclusion in Illinois to enjoy some inspiring scenery.

"Maybe you all could route your trip back where we could meet somewhere...we are off next weekend," Rona wrote.

My heart skipped several beats! I absolutely wanted to meet but didn't want to initiate the idea. I was thrilled that she also was interested in more than an online relationship. Plans came together quickly. We were fortunate that Tennessee was open at the time. We met in Gatlinburg on May 23, 2020. Traffic was light from Georgia to Gatlinburg with fewer travelers on the road that particular Memorial Day weekend. We pulled into the parking lot of the Appy Lodge, uncertain as to who would be the first to arrive. I felt calm and relaxed, or so I thought.

I've learned through the years that I don't always know when my "nerves are on edge." I became masterful at keeping feelings at bay. Imagine all those rumbling, tumultuous thoughts tossing around inside, while I figured I was handling things well and not getting anxious, worried, or nervous. What my body has taught me is that while I'm cool and collected on the outside, my feelings are wreaking havoc on the inside. These feelings eventually become evident by sending my stomach into a bloated mess, making me look like I am four-months pregnant. I camouflage the situation with a flowing, loose top.

As we walked toward the entrance, the automatic doors opened, and a man walked out. He gave me a long look as if he recognized me. I didn't recognize him but quickly noted that I had no idea what Rona's husband Joe looked like. My thoughts fired in rapid succession: *Do I know him? Is this Rona's husband? Is he just being friendly? This is the south! Do I say hello? Do I say nothing? Do I keep walking? WHAT DO I DO???*

I gave a polite half-smile with an "I don't know you- but maybe I should" long glance and then began to walk through the door. This gentleman paused and looked back toward his wife, Rona, whom I recognized. We met for the first time with me entering the hotel and her exiting. *Do we go in, out, hug, not hug? It is the middle of Covid-19, what's the protocol?*

We ended up outside making introductions. Mark and Joe shook hands, Rona and I hugged. The exchange was awkward but at the same time felt right, like a sigh of relief to document that this moment had finally happened. After living just 130 miles apart in the same state for a short time while we were children, each unaware that the other existed, we met and began to get to know each other as siblings. After we checked into our rooms, we had a long conversation as we sat outside on the patio of the hotel. I don't remember much of it, if any! There were so many names and associations that I didn't know and couldn't keep straight in my mind. It was like drinking from a fire hydrant. What mattered was that we had finally met.

Laura

On July 14, 2020, I wrote to Rona, "Do you know a Laura B.?"

Rona replied, I don't think so, should I?"

"I just got on Ancestry to see our connection. We share forty-seven segments (you and I). I share sixty-four segments with a Laura B."

Rona wrote, "Hmmm…that's interesting, I'll look to see if I have anything on mine with that name."

"Shared DNA with Laura is 1726 Dm."

"Ours is 1495."

"Yes."

"You were the first to come up on my closest relatives," Rona pointed out.

"I Sent her a message (through Ancestry), so we'll see what happens…."

On July 15, 2020, I asked Rona, "What did you think about Laura? Did you see her on your Ancestry page?"

Rona answered, "She wasn't on mine."

"Strange."

"Yes. Did she message you back?"

"No. But don't you have to sign into Ancestry? You don't get an automatic email with each new connection, do you?"

Rona said, "No, I don't think so."

I asked, "Maybe I should send a Facebook message?"

She answered, "Wouldn't hurt…I'm intrigued by this."

"Me too!"

On July 15, 2020, I gave it a shot. I Facebook messaged, "Hi Laura, I just noticed on Ancestry that we are closely related…I'm wondering how that might be and would love to figure it out."

Three hours later, she replied, "I would be very interested. I was adopted as an infant. With Covid going on, I haven't pushed the issue, but I should really look into my ancestry seriously."

I wrote, "I was also adopted, but not until the age of two. My birthmother kept me and my brother and then placed us in an orphanage. Do you know anything about your birth parents? I think we might have the same birthfather."

Laura wrote, "I know very little. Most of my records are still sealed as a baby born mid-sixties."

"What year were you born?"

"1965. You?"

"1961."

Laura asked, "I saw the match was very high probability of either father or child. I've never had a child, so… Where are you from?"

"I was born in Trenton. Same birth father, pretty certain."

Laura wrote, "The papers I do have say he was discharged from the Army (honorably), divorced, and not ready to start a family with my birth mother."

I explained, "I don't think he was in the army…It's a bit of a sticky situation…he was not divorced…he was married to the same person (not my birth mother) from 1960 until his death in 2006."

Laura wrote, "Oooh. Yeah. Sticky."

"Yes, sticky, because there are other half-siblings."

Laura asked, "Have you found your birth mother? I was actually shocked on finding my (probably) father. Figured I would find my mother first."

I wrote, "I found her over twenty-five years ago. I actually have my original birth certificate since I was not placed for adoption until two years old."

"That's great. I'm glad for you. I hope I'm as lucky. I was placed in a foster home and then with my [adoptive] parents at four weeks."

"I hope you find answers … there's nothing simple and easy about adoption at any age. It's a lot to sort through."

Laura wrote, "I'm fortunate to know her last name. My adoptive father was a minister, and the agency I was adopted through was affiliated with our church. I think someone overlooked crossing out the names on my paperwork. Thank you for reaching out to me. I am nervous, excited, apprehensive, and scared shitless. Lol. But now I must retire, I get up at 2:30 a.m. for work. We will talk again!"

My mind was spinning. This wasn't the news I wanted to hear, at least not that this new half sibling is four years younger than I am, but more so, I was concerned for Rona. Her head had been spinning since all this began to unravel. It's one thing to find older siblings, quite another to find them younger and born four years into your parents' marriage. I decide not to bring up the subject with Rona. I would wait until she asked about it. I thought that we may be together again when the subject came up, and I could gently tell her face to face about Laura and when she was born.

Of course, that's not what happened. Rona sent a message the following day. On July 16, 2020, Rona wrote, "So, did Laura respond to your FB message?"

"Yes. Adopted as an infant four weeks old!"

"OMGOSH. Wow! So how old is she?"

I wrote, "Well, I wish I could be with you in person...she was born in 1965."

Rona asked, "So, what's your take on this situation?"

"Well, we don't have the same mother. Edith left for California shortly after she put us in the orphanage. What are you thinking?"

"I don't know. I thought your mom may have had other children when she went to California. When were you and Carl adopted? Where was Laura adopted?"

I wrote, "Laura was born in Michigan, adopted there too. Edith married in California and had a son with her husband there."

"What year did she go to California?"

"1963? Edith had told me that she left for California after she placed us in the orphanage."

Mark was sitting in the living room with me as I messaged back and forth with Rona. We commented about how hard it must be to learn that your father had another child after he married your mom, and after you were born. I had a sinking feeling in my gut, an all-over sense of sadness and compassion for what she must have been feeling. I wanted to reach through messenger and give her a hug. She was indeed in denial and grabbing at straws to figure out how Laura was *not* Connor's child."

Rona messaged, "Hmmm...that's a mystery then. How old is your half-brother with your mom and her husband?"

I thought to myself, *Wait a minute. I think Laura said she KNOWS her birthmother's name ... even has it on a document.* I quickly sent Laura a message, "You know your birthmother's name? May I ask what it is? And what church or orphanage?"

She answered, "Last name Ferguson. Was through Lutheran Social Services."

I thought, *WHAT???????* and typed to Rona, "OMG! I think you're right! Laura just told me her [birthmother's] last name is Ferguson, Edith's last name. And I'm so glad Connor is not her father!"

I wrote to Laura, "Hold on. Are you sure?" Now I was the one grabbing at straws, as if she weren't sure of the name on the document she held. I thought we had the same birthfather, but now realized we have the same birthmother. "Do you know your birthfather's name?"

Laura wrote, "No. NO. My records indicate 'mother only parent.' So, I'm assuming she named me before she (we) left the hospital and [she] gave me her last name."

I wrote, "That's my birthmother's last name."

Laura wrote, "Say what?"

"Yep." I momentarily broke away from Laura to read a message from Rona.

Rona wrote, "So, Edith must have gone back to Michigan for a short while after she went to California. Maybe that's why your mom wouldn't answer your questions."

I agreed, "She has so many secrets! She told me she left for California "after we were placed." I guess five years later is technically "after." And I was worried for you because I thought Laura and I had the same father!"

Rona wrote, "I feel for you...that your mom wasn't upfront about it...but I guess I can't say anything because Daddy wasn't either...."

This newest revelation was so much to absorb. I crawled into bed that evening and lay in the stillness. I shouted into the darkness, to no one in particular, "What the fork!" (If you've seen *The Good Place,* you might be chuckling). I tossed and turned, unable to quiet my mind and body to bring on sleep. All this time, all those years that I had known Edith, she never told me the whole story! I didn't wait long before I sent her a text message. It seemed the safest, least confrontational way to approach the subject.

On July 29, I texted, "Hi there, hope you are well. Mark and I submitted DNA for Ancestry about a year ago. Just recently, a match was posted to my DNA...a sister, born 2/18/1965 (Laura B.). The name on her original paperwork says Donna M. Furguson. The paperwork probably slipped through the cracks. She is a lovely woman who would like to get in touch with you. She reached out on Facebook, but I'm guessing you might not check it too often. If you have questions, I'll do my best to answer. Be well." I gave her Laura's email address and phone number.

I received a reply shortly after that read, "Have no idea who this person might be. You have two brothers."

I gasped when I read that. I was beside myself with shock, disappointment, and anger. How could she possibly deny another child? By two brothers, did she mean Connor's sons or Carl and Ben, her son with her current husband? I asked for clarification.

She wrote back, "Carl and Ben."

I replied, "So, here's how ancestry works. When you share DNA, it shows up in Centimorgans (cM). The higher the cM the closer the relationship. Connor had five children that we know of. Doug born in 1957, Carl -1959, Reid-1960, Me-1961, Rona-1961. All different mothers except for me and Carl. I share 1495 cMs with Rona, 1674 cMs with Reid and 1726 cMs with Laura. Laura does not appear on Reid or Rona's Ancestry, so we do not have the same father. She was born in Michigan, at Wayne County General Hospital. Her mother was twenty-three years old, five feet, three inches tall and had three older siblings, all married. Last name Ferguson was given on her paperwork.

She was placed in foster care after she was released from the hospital and then with her adoptive family at four weeks old. I don't think there's any other explanation. It's quite possibly a secret not even your family knew about, maybe your current husband doesn't even know…and it's not mine to tell. I do know she would love to hear from her birth mother."

Edith wrote, "Wow. Didn't know about Doug and Rona. But could have forgotten. This girl is a surprise to me also. Don't remember that. And I think that would be hard to forget. Don't have an explanation. And while we're texting, did I tell you they don't think I really had lupus? (She's been treated for lupus for forty-five years.) Also, I have been fighting pancreatitis for the last three months …."

YES, having a baby would be almost impossible to forget! It's been almost thirty years since my youngest son was born. I may not recall all the details, but I certainly remember being pregnant and giving birth. Maybe if you tell yourself it didn't happen, "I didn't have a baby, I didn't have a baby and leave the hospital without her, I didn't give an infant up for adoption," maybe if you tell yourself those lies over and over for years, you begin to believe them. Maybe.

I felt a hazy mist had been lingering, making it impossible to clearly see and understand all the issues surrounding my birthmother's life decisions. As more and more information surfaced, I began to get an image of a very troubled teenager and young adult. She was likely not well grounded with the ability to learn from previous experiences. She has likely carried her maladaptive behaviors into adulthood. How else can you explain the denial of a child born to you when the evidence is clear and undeniable?

On another level, I feel sad for her. I'm sad that she is not, even after all these years, in a place where she is able to own her past and acknowledge a daughter's existence. Acknowledging Laura would accomplish two things. One, it would give Laura a nugget of validation. It might say to her, "I am worthy of acknowledgment, worthy of being loved, worthy of being remembered. It would say (in Laura's own words), "All I really wanted from the get-go is for someone to say 'Yeah, I had you. I couldn't do it on my own and wanted better for you than I could provide. I never thought I would have to fight for the recognition that I just wasn't found under a cabbage leaf.'" Two, it would, I believe, give Edith some inner peace and allow her body to rest, take a breath, and relax from all the years of hiding. How much emotional and even physical energy has she been exerting for decades in order to keep this secret? I can only imagine the emotional and physical healing she would invite into her body if she would release herself from captivity.

My feelings are mixed. I have anger, exasperation, and disbelief along with sadness toward Edith. My anger is on behalf of Laura. I want to fight for her, to confront Edith and to nudge her once again to contact Laura. When Edith initially denied that she was Laura's birthmother, Laura decided to write her a letter. She mailed it to me, and I sent it along to Edith. I could have divulged all of Edith's contact information, phone, address, and email, but I didn't. I felt that she would appreciate not being blindsided and never imagined that she would completely deny her maternal connection to Laura.

Edith received the letter. I followed up via text message three weeks after mailing it to her. Her response?

"It was well written. Not sure if I will respond."

I replied, "I met Laura in Michigan several weeks ago…lovely woman…she has your eyes. When she talks, she reminds me of you. Her birth father must have been very tall, as she's taller than I am. Having met her, I believe she just wants some validation that yes, her birthmother remembers her. It's something just about every adoptee feels. It might also be healing for you to bring to light what has been hidden for a long time. I believe our bodies pay the price for all the emotional stuff we keep inside or want to forget. I hope you decide to respond, for both of you."

No response.

Introductions

Now, over a year later after introducing Laura and Edith, I'm thinking seriously about giving Laura Edith's contact information. Laura deserves to be seen and heard, not erased like chalk on a chalk board. Just a short time after Edith's denial Laura was able to connect with her birthfather (David) through Ancestry. I was thrilled for her, especially that she was acknowledged by and able to connect with at least one of her birthparents. I was also curious about what information David might have about Edith during this time period. What did he know about her life and her past? David agreed to chat. We met via Zoom and talked about his brief relationship with Edith.

David had the relationship with Edith two years after she placed my brother and me in the orphanage. He told me the following:

> *I always knew her as Edie. I was twenty-four when we met. I was married before my relationship with Edie to a woman who told me she was pregnant…she wasn't. She [actually] became pregnant two months after we married. We had been divorced for a year when I met Edie.*
>
> *We met at the laundry mat where she worked. She also had a part-time job at a drive-in restaurant.*
> *Edie was fun, petite with curly strawberry blonde hair, bubbly, upbeat and friendly. She liked to drink, and I went along with that quite well. I cut a dashing figure at six-feet-four inches tall. I looked good in her convertible. I think she used me a little as eye candy.*

It was a short but torrid relationship that lasted only about four or five months. She was living in Plymouth, Michigan, in a rooming house with several other people.

Her folks lived in Ann Arbor at the time. I only spoke to them one time. We pulled up beside their house in Edie's convertible, they were in the yard, and I spoke to them, but it was primarily Edie speaking to her parents, arguing about something.

I was just an afterthought.

I didn't know anything about you or your brother. It was never discussed. She never brought it up, which is unusual because she knew about my son with my first wife.

While we were seeing each other, I received a draft notice for the armed services. They weren't taking men with children at the time, so it was unusual that I was drafted as a father at the age of twenty-five. I always attributed this anomaly to my ex-wife's grandfather who served on the draft board.

I told Edie and another young lady about the draft notice. I wasn't exclusive with Edie, and she wasn't exclusive with me; it was a relationship of convenience and need. Edie asked me to evade the draft and go to California with her. I told her that wouldn't work since I didn't have a job. But she assured me that I wouldn't have to work. She would support us. I couldn't do something like that and so I left for the service.

Not long after entering the service in August 1964, Edie contacted the US Army and told my commanding officer she was pregnant, and the baby was mine. We were not exclusive, so I wasn't sure. I was gun-shy about young ladies telling me they were pregnant. I told them I had to see a bump before I believed it. Edie hadn't told me she was pregnant [and that that was why she] wanted me to evade the draft and go with her to California. She was two months pregnant when I left, but I didn't know it. My commanding officer told me he could give me leave to "go home and marry that girl," but I told him, "I could go home and NOT marry that girl. You can't make me marry someone."

He got flustered and said "I can order you to," but I told him, "No, you can't." He didn't know quite how to handle the pushback and asked, "Well, now what am I going to do?"

I replied, "She wrote to you, so you must respond." Apparently, he did.

I never saw Edie again or knew where she was.

I knew that Edie had a child, but didn't know if it was mine. We weren't together that long. Thanks to Ancestry, I found Laura, and it was a great surprise.

When I returned from Vietnam, I found that another woman had been pregnant with my child, and she gave the child up for adoption. Apparently, I was very prolific. It was the sixties, passionate, the pill existed, but people didn't use it. I hadn't seen her in three years, and we rekindled our friendship. I'm still searching for the girl she placed for adoption. I have another son from a third young woman (he is younger than Laura). His birthmother raised him on her own.

Newfound Siblings

Unlike Moses, except for my biological brother, I did not live among "my people." Searching for my people, the place where I fit, my tribe, seemed like the most natural thing to do. As it turned out, my tribe was also looking for me. I asked the three siblings I met in 2020 if they would write a few words about their experience through this journey, and they were gracious enough to agree.

From Reid:

When I was younger, eight or nine years old, my uncle John (who was drunk most of the time) used to tell me, "Raymond's not your real father." I also heard this from several of my cousins. When you hear this a dozen or more times at this young age, it makes you wonder. When I was thirteen or fourteen, I was snooping around in my parents' dresser drawer while they were out for the evening. I found a birth certificate that had the name Reid Connor Mumford, born December 1, 1960. That is my birthdate, but my name is Reid Martin with no middle name.

I remember asking my mother why I didn't have a middle name. She said, "It's because your dad doesn't have one." My dad, the one who raised me, the man I love dearly, is named Raymond Martin Jr. It never occurred to me until long after this conversation to ask them why I am not Raymond Martin III.

Mom and Dad's wedding anniversary is four years after my date of birth. So, when I was twenty, they were having their 16th wedding anniversary. I don't know why I never quizzed them about it. I remember asking my mom one time if I was adopted. I was probably about thirteen. She said, "What do you think?" The three of us were sitting in the living room, and I said, "No." It was the last we spoke of it until I was fifty-five years old. It seems like everyone knew but me. Maybe I didn't want to know, or was ashamed, embarrassed, or didn't think it was important. A part of me didn't think it was my place to ask more questions, and that it would have somehow been disrespectful. It's hard to put my finger on it.

My mother decided that the whole situation was weighing heavy on her heart and that she needed to tell me the truth. We sat down in her kitchen, and she told me that Raymond was not my biological father. My biological father was Connor Mumford, a man she met in Chicago. He was from West Virginia. I don't know why they didn't stay together. I think it may have been because he was drinking a lot at the time. I immediately went home after this kitchen conversation and started a Google search for "Connor Mumford." I was nervous and anxious about what I might find. His obituary popped up on the screen, and this is how I found Rona (Connor's daughter and my half-sister).

So, here I am fifty-six years old and finding out that I have a half-sister. I reached out to her and initially, she wasn't too receptive. We became Facebook friends and chatted a few times, and gradually she warmed up to the idea of me being her sibling. Then came the other shock in March 2020. Rona told me that we have another half-sister and two half-brothers. Not only was this a shock, but I also felt deprived of never knowing them. I'm happy that now I have someone in my life to call brother and sister. We found each other right before Covid-19 so we have not spent much time together, but hopefully that will change very soon. Both my newly found sisters are fantastic people with healthy, loving families. I can't wait to know them better and introduce them to my whole family. What a blessing.

From Rona:

Every. Single. Day. That was how often I wished for a brother and sister while I was growing up. At one point, in my younger years, I thought that was going to be the case. When I was thirteens, I asked mother if she was ever going to have any more children. She told me that she and my dad didn't want any more children because, financially, they were working very hard to provide for me to have the things I needed and wanted. Then, she gave me a glimmer of hope. She told me that I might have a brother "out there somewhere."

Before she and Daddy married, he told her that he might have a son, but he wasn't sure if he was his or not. My mother, being the unselfish woman that she was, told my father if he thought the child was his, they could raise him as their own. My father told her he didn't have any idea where the child might even be. So, the times being as they were, they didn't pursue finding him. So I gave up the idea of having siblings. Until...

When I was fifty years old, I was at work in a nursing management position. I was starting my day as usual by opening my emails. There was an unfamiliar sender in my inbox. Our corporation had warned us about opening emails from unfamiliar senders, but my curiosity overcame me, and I opened the email. I began to read it and couldn't believe what I was reading. A possible sister? It couldn't be. I had so many mixed emotions; ones of surprise, ones of doubt, ones of hope. It had been a few years since my father had passed away, and my mother was still in such a deep depression from his passing. I just couldn't ask her about this right now, as I was still dealing with my own closure of my father's passing. I responded to the email, but I had reservations. The sender and I exchanged several emails and left it between us that I would email her back when I was ready to discuss more things with her. She knew some things about my father, but couldn't anyone in this day and time find out information through internet research?

Then, about two years later, I received an email from another unfamiliar sender. I decided to open this one as well. This email was from a man who was asking if my father had grown up in West Virginia, knew some men, whose names I can't remember at this point, and if my father had lived in Chicago as a young adult. I thought maybe one of the men didn't know my father had passed away and that maybe he was trying to catch up on old times. I asked my mother. She thought she remembered my father mentioning the names, but she wasn't sure. So, I responded to the email and to my amazement, the sender informed me that he may be my brother! I thought maybe he was the son my father had told my mom about before they were married. The woman who had emailed me had mentioned that she had a brother but didn't say if they were in contact with each other. Could this be him? So, I finally decided to ask my mother if she knew about the woman. She told me the story.

Evidently, not long after I was born, the woman (Edith) who was the birthmother of the woman who had emailed me (Terri), contacted my father's mother, and informed my grandmother that she had given birth to a boy and a girl. Both belonged to my father. She wanted to meet my grandmother and bring the children to meet her.

The woman's intent was to ask my grandmother to raise the children. However, after meeting my grandmother, she decided that was not the best idea (that's another story in and by itself). So, my grandmother told my father about the children after they had visited and returned back to Michigan. He never heard anything else about the children.

But that boy was not the child that my father had told my mother about before they got married. So how many possible siblings does that make? One boy (Doug) that he had told my mom about, the boy (Carl) and girl (Terri) that their mother had brought to meet my grandmother, and the other boy that my mother did not know about (Reid). So, were there four?

Then, in 2020, I received a Facebook message from a young lady asking me if my father was from West Virginia and other questions that were indicative that she knew information about my family. I asked myself if this was another sibling. After messaging, it was evident that she was my niece (daughter of Doug). Unfortunately, Doug had passed away the previous year. She was trying to make connections through people she had heard him mention. She had a younger sister, and they both wanted to meet me. After confirmation of the information that she shared, I told her about the other probable siblings. We all ended up submitting to Ancestry DNA, and it was confirmed that we were related through my father.

All this information was overwhelming in the beginning, but now I feel so blessed that God has brought us all together. Since that time, I have met all but one of my brothers. When meeting Terri for the first time, I saw my father's gentle, quiet, and observing demeanor that brought about his wisdom. When meeting Reid for the first time, I saw my father's strength and quick wit. I also met the daughters of Doug and saw the inquisitive nature that my father had. I hope for all of us to have a family get together with all the children of my father and their families one day. I couldn't be happier for the family that I always wanted to have. And I can't thank Terri enough for being patient with me as I needed to reconnect in my own time.

From Laura:

Searching my earliest childhood memories, I cannot remember a time not knowing I was adopted. My parents never attached any negative connotation to that fact. Instead, they made every effort to let me know that they "chose" me to be their child. The stigma came when I told my friends. They became almost apologetic. I even had some ask if I was treated differently by my parents. Finding my humor early in life, I would run with that story until I couldn't keep a straight face.

As a small child, I felt proud that my parents picked me to be a part of their family. I suppose I was rather sheltered growing up with a minister for a father. In the early seventies there seemed to be an almost protected status that I enjoyed. Maybe that had something to do with having an overprotective older brother, but either way, not much attention was given to the fact that he and I were adopted. Little kids have fewer questions than bigger kids and adults. We were just happy to play with our friends.

My teen years were somewhat trying, as most are. I remember some resentment towards my biological parents (especially my mother). I felt inadequate and placed the blame on myself, as if I could have somehow changed the situation or outcome. As a college student, I sent my name and info to a registry in hopes that a parent had possibly submitted his or hers. This was, of course, before the internet. Knowing that adoption records were sealed prior to 1970, I didn't expect to have much luck. I didn't pursue it any further for a time, as I began questioning whether or not I really wanted to know. You second guess yourself. If they were any kind of parent at all, how could they not want to know what happened to me? Do they even care if I'm alive or if a family even opened their hearts to take me in? Maybe they just threw me out with the trash, never to think about me again.

Oh, how the mind runs through all the scenarios of "What If." What if I was a result of a traumatic relationship or at worst, a forced encounter or rape? How old was my mother? Was she sixteen and still a child herself? Did she want to keep me but was forced to give me up so she could pursue more opportunities than that of an unwed mother? Was she still in the area? Imagine walking into a store and wondering if the person you lock eyes with is related to you? Then, someone tells you that you have a twin working at the store near you. Do you investigate? If you find them, do you approach them?

How many times do you need to hear, "Who did you get your brown eyes from?" or, "Who do you look like?" And you answer all the questions, silly or not. For so many people it's an eye-opening discussion. I welcome the questions. I'll never discourage a discussion about adoption. I'll never turn down an opportunity to educate someone about adoption, at least from an adoptee's perspective. Sometimes it amazes me what kind of information and opinions people have on the subject.

My adult years were spent buried in work—a self-inflicted condition to ward off the loneliness and abandonment issues. With work occupying sixty to eighty hours per week, little time is left to form personal or romantic relationships. I was scared to death of getting involved with someone and possibly creating a life in which I may have to choose whether to keep and raise a child or place a child for adoption as I had been. I did not want to perpetuate the cycle that had been so difficult to deal with. How could I subject another human being to the turmoil I suffered? How could I make the hardest decision of my life? Could I make that right decision?

As an adult, I wrestled with feelings of inadequacy, of constantly wanting to please everyone (especially the women and mother figures in my life). I beat myself up when I thought I had let someone down, falling into dark depressions for days or weeks and hiding behind a huge wall of denial.

Then came a job change! Working twenty hours fewer per week gave me time for a LIFE. I certainly wasn't prepared for that! More free time and a good friend who took special interest in my mental health, meant I was gearing up to face all my long-buried issues. I had built the wall so high, it took a while for that friend to convince me to seek help.

Not long into the therapy sessions I realized that I harbored some resentment toward my mother. This is probably quite common; in having conversations with other adoptees, we seem to have similar stories. Interestingly, I did not have the same resentment toward my father. What a burden to saddle a woman with! Not only does she make the ultimate decision to complete a pregnancy, but then she also has to choose to give up all rights and contact with a living being she cared for and carried for nine months.

A year or more into therapy, I finally let down my guard a little bit and opened myself up to seeking a romantic relationship. Still scared of rejection and abandonment, I wouldn't let myself trust too much. After several attempts at letting someone get close and then putting up the wall again, I found my forever partner. He accepts me and my baggage. I could not ask for a more supportive husband. Quite often, he's pushing me to take the next step, whether I'm ready or not.

Now, along came the internet and then some sophisticated DNA testing. Do I try it? That old feeling of fear and doubt start creeping in. What if ….? What if my parents are already dead? What if nobody else has submitted DNA? What if I find family and nobody wants to admit to my existence? What if I get rejected … again?

As it was, I submitted my sample at the onset of the Covid 19 pandemic, so it was a while before my results became available. Well, as they say, the results don't lie. Not knowing quite how to read the website, I figured most of the results I was seeing were extended family. One day, out of the blue, I decided to check my DNA site messages. There it was. A message. "Hi! We share a lot of DNA. I'd like to figure out how we're related." Absolutely unprepared for that, my heart raced (first, a good race, then a bad race). I giggled. I cried a lot. I got scared. Really scared.

My support system (my husband) wanted to know what my major malfunction was. I wished I knew what to tell him. I wanted to know more, but I didn't want to throw my whole heart into the frying pan and have it burst into flames. Of course, he's a guy, so he said, "What's the problem? Just do it!" Easy for him to say.

Well, after a few more days of self-doubt, I jumped in headfirst. Messaging back and forth, we realized how we are related. Wow! I have a sister! I have a blood relative! I have other relatives! She was under the impression that we shared the same father. I happened to have paperwork from the agency that I was placed through, and it included mostly non-identifying information about my birth and some generic family background. It also included a page with my given name I had when I left the hospital. The papers were signed by "mother and only parent," so I assumed that she had given me her last name.

When I told my sister that I knew my mother's maiden name and what it was, I'm pretty sure she came close to falling off her chair. As she has met our biological mother, she was shocked to find out she had another sibling from her mother's side. She revealed to me that our mother is still alive. I also learned that she has no desire to acknowledge me. So … the high, then the low. The acceptance and the rejection. It was crazy how fast my sister and I connected and decided to meet in person. We started messaging in mid-July, and by mid-August we were planning the trip to meet. Of course, I almost threw up on the whole three-hour ride over. I can honestly say I have never had such an immediate connection with someone as I did that day. We discussed everything we could think of in the short time we had.

She suggested I write a letter to our mother, which I did. I tried to be as accepting as possible. To no avail. She admitted to my sister that I wrote a "nicely written letter," but she did not respond or acknowledge anything. I'm disappointed that I might not have the chance to meet with my biological mother and let her know that I am, for the most part, okay. If it's not going to be any sort of relationship, I'd at least like a meeting for closure on my part. As it stands, I'm not sure I could handle being rejected, again.

That disappointment was outweighed by the newest development. There was a DNA match that said *parent/child*. Knowing I have never had any children, I stared at a message from my biological father with only one question. "Can I ask? Were you adopted?" I told him yes and he came back telling me he was my father. After confirming my mother's name, we covered the dates and locations of my birth and adoption and talked about other generalities. Not two weeks went by, and we were meeting in person. He had submitted his DNA some time ago and was looking for me and another child that he had lost contact with. He was especially eager to relate some health history, as none of us are getting any younger and figured I probably had no knowledge of any of it.

It was a very comfortable visit, like meeting up with an old friend. Now he wants to introduce me to extended family, and I want to do the same. I want him to know what a great family and support system I had growing up and, also what I have now. He's eager to meet my parents, as they are to meet him.

The stories of his youth and young adult years continue to interest me. I'm eager to glean all the information I can about our family history and how he met my mother. He still talks about her fondly. Even with only one side of the story, it's better than not knowing anything at all.

I'm glad I had the upbringing I did, and my parents let me decide on my own how I felt about the whole situation. They never put negative thoughts in my head. Adoption was always talked about in a positive light. My folks were just happy that they got to adopt a daughter to raise, as they were to adopt my brother before me, and this was after having a child by natural birth. They were generous enough to open their hearts and home to us, not knowing either of our backgrounds or situations. I've met people who wouldn't even consider adoption, as they don't want to raise 'someone else's problem.' I get it. I understand. My brother still fights his demons he grew up with. He added a few gray hairs to my folks' heads. Not that I probably didn't, also. I am happy that at almost sixty, my brother has done a complete 180 and decided to submit his DNA to find what family he may have out there. I pray his news is nothing but positive.

I am intrigued when I hear people discuss how they found birth families, extended families, and distant relatives. When the topic of adoption comes up, I love listening to the different stories and I will tell mine whenever I can. One thing I ask. Don't apologize when I tell you I'm adopted. There's nothing to be sorry for. I was raised by wonderful parents. I have two great brothers. I had wonderful grandparents. I was a kid, a teenager, a young adult and am an all-around normal person. I've also been fortunate to meet a biological parent. Don't apologize to me. Apologize to all the children stuck in the system and living in orphanages or foster homes all their lives. Apologize to the children who will never know a permanent stable home environment. Rejoice with me that I have found some family members and have the knowledge that I am not alone in this world. I have my family. They will always be my family. I have my kids, grandkids, and great grandkids. I love them all! And now, I have the knowledge of blood relatives I will get to know and add to my family. I am truly blessed.

This simple diagram shows complex connections
between my siblings and me.

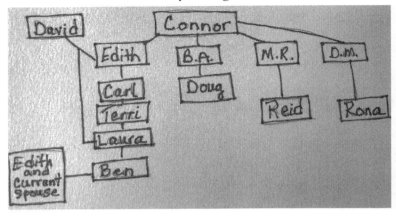

Solid Ground

I asked my brother Carl about memories because I often doubted my own. I remembered watching as he got his mouth washed out with soap. But did it really happen? Is that an accurate memory? He shared some of his memories in a letter; he has his own deep feelings about not belonging. It amazes me that we never talked about adoption. Not as children, not as adolescents, not as adults, not until I started digging around in the emotional cellar when he was well into his fifties.

The shame and secrecy that can surround adoption is astounding and a change we must set in motion for the emotional health of all those in the adoption constellation. Not all adoptive families have an unspoken code of silence. I know a few who talk openly, painfully, and authentically about the many facets of a complicated life history. Unfortunately, I think this is rare.

It was heart wrenching and painful to read about my brother's emotional scars. To respect his privacy, it's something that will remain between him and me.

I imagine that writing a book about my adoption experience might come as a shock to family members accustomed to silence surrounding the topic. They may be asking, *How could she? What's wrong? Why is she writing? What is she writing? How am I going to be portrayed? Why isn't she just grateful?*

When my father was ill, I made periodic calls home to see how he was doing. Mom is always chatty, even if things aren't going well. One particular day in late August, she was different.

"Hi Mom"

"Hi." She replied.

Then silence …

"How are you?" I asked.

"Okay." More silence. This never happens and I wondered what was going on.

"How's Dad?"

"Pretty good." Again, silence. She broke the monosyllabic response, but still, I sensed something wasn't quite right.

"I just wanted to call and check on Dad to see how he was feeling."

"About the same," she replied. Another long silence.

"Well, I was just checking in. I'll call back when it's a better time."

She quickly said, "Carl called."

"Okay" I said, confused as to what that could possibly have to do with the purpose of my call. To my knowledge, their relationship had been distant for years. I wasn't even aware that he kept any contact with them at all.

She continued, "He said you told him he was abused, and you are writing a book about it."

"What?" Not because I didn't hear her, but because I couldn't believe my ears. Now all the silence made sense. "No. I did not tell Carl any such thing. I asked him about memories. I am writing a book about adoption—mine and Maya's. That is exactly what I told Carl." Somewhere in the ensuing conversation I tried to explain to her what it might be like for a child to be taken away from her home. Remember, she and I have never discussed, on any level, the feelings around adoption.

"Mom, imagine if John (her adult grandson) and Emily (his wife) were to one day say to their two-year-old son Jaden that he was going to get a new mom and dad, and then they sent him off with a complete stranger. Can you even begin to imagine what that would do to him?"

"Well," she replied, "you're not a two-year-old. You're an adult."

My heart, soul, and everything within me began to sink. For some reason unknown to me, she doesn't get it, doesn't see it, and probably never will. I realized in that instant it was futile to try any further. In that conversation, one of her comments that stuck with me was, "Things haven't been right between us for some time." I had no idea she felt that way and no idea what circumstances led her to that statement. This speaks to the lack of open, honest communication that characterized our family. From my perspective, compliance was expected. There was no tolerance for complicated, difficult, uncomfortable emotions. You go along to get along. Period.

The silent treatment she gave me in those brief moments early in the phone call spoke volumes. I made a monumental decision. I needed to set some boundaries (something I had never done). I decided that I would not let her treat me with such passive-aggressive behavior. I would not call. I would communicate via email. It felt much safer.

About six weeks later, my dad entered hospice care. Mom never called to tell me. My brother-in-law did. Well, not exactly, he called my husband and told him. I did not go see Dad. I felt the phone call was merely informative, a courtesy, and not an invitation to visit in his last days. I didn't feel my presence would be wanted or welcomed and would only stir up the most recent misunderstanding and years of unspoken hurt. A few weeks after being in hospice, Dad passed away. Mom never called to tell me.

Once again, my brother-in-law called. He also reprimanded me (though he wouldn't call it that) via email the day after the funeral, writing, "Your almost total absence from Shelbyville the past four months was startling. Until this week I had talked with your mom about it one time and she referred to the same phone call you told me about and with about the same number of specifics. Mary and I discussed it from time to time. 'It was a shame,' we would say, but we didn't understand it. Rather than let it become a further divide between us, I decided to reach out to you. Mary isn't part of that, but she knows I am doing it.

I have no idea what has gone on, lately or long ago. I don't doubt your pain. Absent some dark secret that I don't know, I would have expected to see you with your dad more. Please do not take this as an accusation or attempt to produce guilt."

The funeral service directly followed the visitation. There was seemingly no plan for the visitation as far as where we were supposed to stand or if we were supposed to greet people at all. People started coming in the back door while the family was gathered at the front near the casket. The chairs in the spacious room were split down the middle. The casket was centered with the aisle and about twelve feet away from the front row. Mary and her husband were on one side of the aisle between the front row and the casket. Mom was on the other with Carl and Cathy. I finally made my way to stand next to Cathy and noticed Trent in the periphery, unsure of what to do. I asked him if he wanted to come and stand next to me.

I noticed how strange it was that Mary, the only biological child, was on one side of the aisle and all the adopted children (except for Neal, who didn't attend) were on the other. Those are the little, or maybe not so little, things that I notice and wonder about. Did it just happen that way, or is there more going on below the surface?

I consider those few months and particularly the phone call incident as the turning point in the relationship with my mom. The undetected storm had been brewing for years beneath all the silence. It only needed a spark to be ignited. Dad passed away four years ago. I continued to write emails to Mom from time to time and got brief replies. If I wrote, she responded, but she did not take initiative to communicate. I began to grow weary of the pattern, sending fewer and fewer emails until I decided to stop the charade. My communication the last two years has been simple. I send a birthday card and a sweet treat at Christmas. I received a note last Christmas thanking me for the sweets. Other than that, I do not hear from her. Not on my birthday, not at Christmas, nothing.

In June, five years after Dad's passing, Mark and I were taking care of our grandsons in Florida while our son and daughter-in-law spent a weekend away to celebrate their anniversary. We were getting ready to crawl into bed when my phone rang. It was a number I didn't recognize, so I didn't answer. The caller left a voicemail, so I listened. I heard my brother Carl.

"This is your brother Carl. Mom died."

"What?" I said to myself, unable to believe what I was hearing. I quickly called Carl back and he confirmed mom's death.

"Yeah, I only found out because Scott (our cousin) stopped by to work on my air conditioning, and he told me Mom was in the hospital. I called Randall [our brother-in-law] this morning to find out what was going on and didn't hear back from him until this evening. He said Mom died this afternoon."

I don't remember much more from our conversation. I do remember crawling into bed and telling my husband, "When Randall calls to tell YOU that my mom died. Tell him to call ME."

Ten minutes later Mark's phone rang. It was Randall. A minute into the conversation Mark said, "Randall, Terri is right here. Why don't you tell her?" and he handed me the phone.

There was no visitation. No funeral. Nothing. That seemed odd to me. Maybe even in death she did not want us around. I don't know. It's a mystery. A few weeks later I called my sister Mary and left a message offering to help sort through the house and all the end-of-life things that must be done when both parents are gone. When Mark's mom passed away, we had all five siblings and their spouses and children together to decide what to do with her possessions. It was a daunting task for twenty-five people! I imagined it must be overwhelming for Mary to have to face this on her own. I didn't offer because there was something I wanted, and I let her know this. I simply wanted to help. I never heard from her. Maybe she never got the message. Several months later I received a small box in the mail with a few photos, an old yearbook, and a note that said, "I thought you might like these photos from Mom's house."

I don't know what it was like to walk in my adoptive mother's shoes. She had five adopted children who all, to some degree, have struggled with attachment and belonging. I have only one, and I know the emotional weight of just that one is at times overwhelmingly exhausting. The difference is that I understand the struggle to attach and connect. I don't hold it against Maya that this is present in our relationship, though I wish it weren't there. I wait, love, accept, get frustrated, wait some more, take steps forward and then backward, wait, love, accept.... The cycle must be repeated.

I'm not interested in an "I'm right and you're wrong" outcome. There really is no right or wrong. What's left? Understanding. We must accept, sympathetically and without judgment, the experience of the other.

I recently attended a dinner where a wide spectrum of adoption was represented at the table. In addition to my adoption and Maya's, a single woman's ex-husband was adopted. Another couple had three biological children and two children adopted internationally at the ages of twelve and thirteen. The remaining couple had no personal experience with the deep waters of adoption that we were discussing and stopped me mid-sentence. The husband asked, "What are the deep waters of adoption?"

The "deep waters" are why I wrote this book and why I feel it's needed for many in the adoption constellation. It's important that we gain insight into others' experiences and perspectives. As an adoptive parent, have I considered that my child might not feel that he or she completely fits and belongs in our family? If so, have I given thought to what this must feel like on a day-to-day basis? As an adoptee, have I considered what it's like for a parent who just wants the adoptee's loss, grief, etc., to melt away now that the child has another family? And what about all the questions between birthmother and relinquished child?

In all my conversations where the subject of adoption comes up, I have met numerous people who share their own connection to adoption either by being an adoptive parent, adoptee, sibling to an adoptee, or other. I have yet to meet a birthmother who shares her story of relinquishment of her child. I don't think this is due to a shortage of birthmothers but due to the shame (and perhaps regret) many of them have carried their whole lives. I understand the desire to remain hidden and anonymous, not wanting to invite the judgment of others. My experience is that we are most harsh and judgmental toward ourselves.

I started this memoir over ten years ago. So much has changed in me and in my relationships through the entire process. Both of my adoptive parents are now deceased. I think our understanding of each other grew cloudy and murky as I began to grow personally and make connections to my own feelings about adoption. I believe in life after death. I have a feeling that on the other side of this life, we'll have a greater understanding of one another.

My birthmother is still living. Still in denial. Still distant. I'm not sure how much would change even if she acknowledged birthing Laura. At least we would have a foundation of truth and openness to build upon. Currently, I can only describe the minimal relationship as awkward.

Maya. It's no secret that mother-daughter relationships can be tumultuous. Layer on the attachment and abandonment issues that often come with adoption, and you may find yourself in the eye of the storm. While this isn't true for every family who adopts, it can be part of the story.

I have tried to give Maya her space, even more so now that she has a family of her own. She is married with an eight-month-old boy. She recently posted a video of herself holding her son and dancing to music. It was rich to watch and touching to see her nurture him in this way, especially since we know little of her early history. I'm thrilled that she can give what she might not have received from her own biological family.

As constellations change over time, so does the adoption constellation. We change as individuals (hopefully). Our understanding, perspective, experience, and insight all have potential for growth.

But it takes work. It's been a challenge to bring this writing to an end for this very reason. There are ongoing insights and understanding to the past and present, which led to more writing!

Adoption is a lifelong journey, not a one-time event. I think and feel differently about my adoption as I grow and change as an individual. My life experiences give me new scenery, new relationships, and new perspective. These experiences have opened my eyes to feelings related to my adoption that I had never known before. I used to tell myself that being adopted didn't matter and didn't bother me, that I was just like any other child in any other family.

Adoption does matter and has had a profound effect on my life. I have also come to understand that forging this relationship between parent and child is a dance, and for that dance to work, there must be movement from both people. We must learn to anticipate each other, work together, sense each other's rhythm and flow, learn when to come closer, and recognize when to allow space. This is all a dance through loss, fear, anger, pain, and whatever other emotions may surface.

Adoptive parents need to understand that there are likely many stages an adopted child may go through. Consequently, parents may also experience many different stages and feelings.

A successful adoption is not one where the adoptee "fits right in" and "has no issues," but rather where communication about difficult and ambivalent feelings is encouraged on a continual basis. Questions should be respected and given age-appropriate answers.

Adoption is a tangled web of emotion. The complexity cannot be overstated. Adopting a child is not a "simple fix" for the plight of the child or the parents. Adoptive parents must, if they haven't already, open their eyes to the difficulties, insecurities, identity issues, anger, shame, etc., that their adopted child may face. Silence about these issues on the child's part does not mean that these issues don't exist. A child may not feel safe enough to express that everything isn't "okay" now that he or she has a "permanent" family.

The parents' never-ending role is to provide a place of safety for their adopted child. And even more important, they must accept the child where he or she is and then show love, hold nothing back (even though the adoptee may always hold back, fearing another rejection).

Don't buy into the idea that adoption, as a means of building a family, "doesn't matter." It matters. We as adoptive parents are responsible for acknowledging, not replacing, the irreplaceable loss our child has experienced. Yes. Irreplaceable. That doesn't mean we don't matter or are insignificant. That *does* mean we are loving substitutes who nurture, understand, and show compassion to the children who now call us Mom and Dad.

Amidst all its complexities, there is beauty in adoption. That beauty is found when we reach beyond ourselves, beyond our assumptions or ideologies, and sit with what it must be like to be adopted, to be a foreigner in another land. When we can acknowledge the loss of an adopted child and be at peace with the possibility that we may not be the complete solution, the dance can begin. I am learning with my own daughter that this dance is beautiful. It hasn't always been easy for either of us, but as Rumi says, "Where there is ruin, there is hope for treasure."

While being a member of the adoption constellation has been challenging, I would not ask for another life experience. This journey has led me to walk solo across Spain as a pilgrim on the Camino de Santiago in 2009, complete a year-long training in the expressive arts in 2015, become a certified yoga instructor in 2018, open my own yoga and art studio, and write a memoir. None of these were on my radar before I began the demanding work of exploring my life story and healing. I'm grateful to understand the depth of loss an adoptee feels. I am blessed to now listen to other adoptees and get it. I appreciate the opportunity to be able to give that level of understanding to someone else.

While sitting on our screened porch this morning and surrounded by the peace of the north Georgia mountains, I noticed a pileated woodpecker. These birds are nothing like the woodpeckers we had in our yard in Illinois. The pileated woodpecker is about the size of a crow, maybe bigger, and fascinating to watch. This woodpecker was perched at the top of a large, bare tree as the sun shone through the bird's red-plumed top, giving the appearance of a tongue of fire resting on its head.

Eventually, the bird took flight, soaring through the air as if it knew its exact destination. I watched as the bird disappeared into the distance. I never saw it land, but I know it did, somewhere.

This is how I see life continuing to unfold, no matter what our experiences have been, in or outside the adoption constellation.

We fly. Sometimes we soar. We land high on a treetop or maybe low in a valley, only to fly again, knowing there will always be a place to learn, to grow, and to land.

Discussion Questions

1) What, if any, ideas surrounding adoption changed and/or expanded as you read this book?

2) How has adoption changed who you are and/or how you are in this world?

3) Where do you notice unspoken rules of silence surrounding adoption in your life?

4) How might adoptive parents be more prepared for the issues they may encounter with their adopted child?

5) How is belonging and connectedness evident in your life?

6) What thoughts or emotions surfaced as you read the analogy comparing adoption to animals caged in the zoo?

7) If you have an adopted child, how have you noticed your child searching for their 'own people'?

8) In your opinion, is it possible to heal the wounds of abandonment and loss experienced early in
9) life/childhood?

10) What do you think prompted the authors decision to walk the Camino across Spain?

11) How have you been touched by adoption?

About the Author

In her candid memoir, Terri addresses the complicated issues of adoption. She draws from her experience as one of five adopted children as well as her experiences as a biological and adoptive mother.

Terri is a certified yoga instructor with training in the expressive arts. She experiments with a variety of artistic mediums, including writing, photography, silk dying, and acrylic pour painting. She loves being in nature, gardening, and hiking. Terri and her husband live in the north Georgia mountains, where they frequently welcome their six beloved grandchildren.

Made in the USA
Columbia, SC
14 October 2022

69441876R00102